Mary of Scotland

Maxwell Anderson

Kessinger Publishing's Rare Reprints

Thousands of Scarce and Hard-to-Find Books on These and other Subjects!

- Americana
- Ancient Mysteries
- Animals
- Anthropology
- Architecture
- Arts
- Astrology
- Bibliographies
- Biographies & Memoirs
- Body, Mind & Spirit
- Business & Investing
- Children & Young Adult
- Collectibles
- Comparative Religions
- Crafts & Hobbies
- Earth Sciences
- Education
- Ephemera
- Fiction
- Folklore
- Geography
- Health & Diet
- History
- Hobbies & Leisure
- Humor
- Illustrated Books
- Language & Culture
- Law
- Life Sciences

- Literature
- Medicine & Pharmacy
- Metaphysical
- Music
- Mystery & Crime
- Mythology
- Natural History
- Outdoor & Nature
- Philosophy
- Poetry
- Political Science
- Science
- Psychiatry & Psychology
- Reference
- Religion & Spiritualism
- Rhetoric
- Sacred Books
- Science Fiction
- Science & Technology
- Self-Help
- Social Sciences
- Symbolism
- Theatre & Drama
- Theology
- Travel & Explorations
- War & Military
- Women
- Yoga
- *Plus Much More!*

We kindly invite you to view our catalog list at:
http://www.kessinger.net

Maxwell Anderson

MARY OF SCOTLAND

MAXWELL ANDERSON

To the honor of having won the Pulitzer Prize for *Both Your Houses* in 1933, Maxwell Anderson can claim the added distinction of having been the first playwright to be awarded the Critic's Circle accolade for *Winterset* in 1936. Born in Atlantic, Pennsylvania, in 1888, Maxwell Anderson received his A.B. degree from the University of North Dakota and his master's degree from Leland Stanford. After a short career as a teacher, he turned to journalism and served successively on the staffs of the *Grand Forks* (North Dakota) *Herald, San Francisco Chronicle, San Francisco Bulletin, New Republic, New York Evening Globe* and *New York Morning World.* His work on the last-named newspaper brought friendship with Laurence Stallings, with whom he collaborated in the writing of the immensely successful *What Price Glory?* Since then Maxwell Anderson has won both critical and public acclaim with such plays as *Elizabeth the Queen* and *Mary of Scotland,* as well as the two dramatic works for which he won the highest honors our country can give.

CHARACTERS

FIRST GUARD, JAMIE
SECOND GUARD
THIRD GUARD
JOHN KNOX
JAMES HEPBURN, Earl of Bothwell
CHATELARD
MARY STUART
DUC DE CHATELHERAULT
MARY BEATON
MARY SETON
MARY LIVINGSTONE
MARY FLEMING
ELIZABETH TUDOR
LORD BURGHLEY
HENRY, LORD DARNLEY
LORD GORDON
DAVID RIZZIO
JAMES STUART, Earl of Moray
MAITLAND of Lethington
LORD HUNTLEY
LORD MORTON
LORD ERSKINE
LORD THROGMORTON
A PORTER
LORD RUTHVEN
LORD DOUGLAS
YOUNG RUTHVEN
FIRST SENTINEL
SECOND SENTINEL
A SERGEANT
A WARDEN
SOLDIERS AND OTHERS

MARY OF SCOTLAND

ACT ONE

SCENE I

SCENE: *A half-sheltered corner of the pier at Leith. It is a sleety, windy night, and the tall piles of the background and the planks underfoot shine black and icy with their coating of freezing rain. Long cables stretch away into the dark. The only light comes from the lantern of two iron-capped* GUARDS *who are playing cards morosely on the head of a fish-tub in the lee of a great coil of rope.*

FIRST GUARD

Na, na, put them away. I'm fair clabbered with the cold.

SECOND GUARD

Aye, you'd say that, wi' ma siller-piece laced in your brogues!

FIRST GUARD

Gie me the hand, then. But man, it's an unco bitter nicht for indoor pleasures.

SECOND GUARD

(*Throwing out cards*). It's a blastit wonner—

FIRST GUARD

Put out, put out!

SECOND GUARD

(*Laying down a coin*). Aye.

FIRST GUARD

And we'll just stop now, forbye to go on 'ud strain your two-year credit. (*He shows his hand.*)

SECOND GUARD

Dod, mon ye hae luck wi' the titties. Ye'll no refuse me ma revenge, Jamie? (*A tall bearded* FIGURE *muffled in a cloak, has come in from the left.*)

FIRST GUARD

When ye can afford it. No earlier.

SECOND GUARD

Ye see yoursel', Jamie. I'm gouged out clean—

FIRST GUARD

And is that a reason I should risk my gains—?

THE OLD MAN

Aye, dicing, gaming, cards, drinking, dancing, whoring, and all the papistical uses of the flesh—they run before 'her like a foul air—

SECOND GUARD

It's the Master—wheesht—put them awa'.

FIRST GUARD

An' what of it? I'm na member of his congregation.
(*A third* GUARD *runs in from the right.*)

THIRD GUARD

I was right, Jamie! 'Tis the queen's ship!

FIRST GUARD

The Queen's ship, you goik! How could it be the queen's ship? She's to come in a galley, and she's none due this month yet.

THIRD GUARD

My word on it, Tod, I rid out wi' the fishermen, and she's a galley wi' oars, and by God she carries the oriflamme!

SECOND GUARD

Would the queen's ship dock without notice to the lords, and no retinue at the pier?

THIRD GUARD

There it lies—yon wi' the lights!

FIRST GUARD

She's lights aplenty, afore God. Aweel, we've no orders aboot it.

THIRD GUARD

Bur we can do no less than give her what escort we can—

FIRST GUARD

We're set to guard the pier, and for nowt else.—And why are you so hot for a Romish sovereign to set foot on Scottish soil, do you mind if I ask?—For myself, I'm no member of the congregation, I'm a sojer doing what I'm set to, but it runs in my head we've had enough of the Guises and their Holy Father. Let them stick to their warm climates where they're welcome— and may they come to a hotter place before they set up another standard here!

THE OLD MAN

Ye may be na member of the congregation, friend, but you will be if you keep in that opinion. For her or against her it's to be in this land, and no half-way to stand on. The kirk of Christ or the hussy of Rome, drowned in wine, bestial with fornication, corrupt with all diseases of mind and blood—

SECOND GUARD

Is it the queen's galley, Master?

THE OLD MAN

Aye, is it.

SECOND GUARD

For there's been no herald of it, nor any one told—

THE OLD MAN

I have my ways of knowing. And, hearing of it, I came myself to see this white face they speak of, and these taking graces, and to tell her to that white face of hers and despite her enchantments that we want and will have none of her here. For whatever beauty she may possess, or whatever winning airs, they are given her of the devil to cozen us, they are born solely of the concupiscence of hell and set upon her like a sign. They say when she speaks she drips honey and she smells sweet with boughten perfumes, but I say the man who tastes of her or the people who trust in her will chew on dry ashes in the last day and find no remedy for that thirst! I say she comes with a milk-white body and a tongue of music, but beware her, for she will be to you a walking curse and a walking death!

THIRD GUARD

You will say this to the queen?

THE OLD MAN

I will say this to her whey face! (BOTHWELL enters from the right.)

BOTHWELL

Leg it over to the inn, one of you lads, and fetch a chair—

FIRST GUARD

We're on guard here, my lord.

BOTHWELL

Damn your guard duty! The queen of Scotland's stepping out of a boat in velvet shoes—

THIRD GUARD

I doubt there's a chair nearer than Edinburgh town—

BOTHWELL

There's one at the Leith inn, as ye well know—

FIRST GUARD

We'd need the silver for that, in any case—

BOTHWELL

My mannie, if I was to lay a fist to the side of that iron pot of yours I doubt the dinge would come out in a hurry—. What the devil do ye mean bauchling over a dirty chair? Seize it, seize it in the queen's name!

THIRD GUARD

I'll fetch it, sir. (He starts out.)

BOTHWELL

And do you go with him. I suspect ye of being a psalm-singer with that face.

(*The first* GUARD *goes with the third.*)
A verra braw evening to you, Master Knox.

THE OLD MAN

And to you, my lord.

BOTHWELL

It seems some here heard of her coming, though not perhaps those she'd have chosen. You're not here, by chance, to greet the daughter of Mary of Guise?

THE OLD MAN

If I have aught to say to her, it will be for her own ears.

BOTHWELL

No doubt, no doubt. And I have a little observe to make to you about that, too, sir. Whatever it is you have to say to her you won't say it.

THE OLD MAN

And why not? Are the Papists muzzling the ministers of God?

BOTHWELL

I'm no Papist, as ye're aware, Master Knox, and if I were I'm no such fool as to try to muzzle a minister, nevertheless, whatever it was you were going to say, you won't say it, that's my observe to you—

KNOX

I shall say what I have come to say.
(BOTHWELL *follows the Soldiers. A man's voice, speaking French in a light tenor, comes in from the right.*)

CHATELARD

(*Outside*). It is a badge of honor, I assure Your Majesty.

MARY

(*Outside*). Still, when next you toss your cloak in the mud, take note whether there are any watching to report it—

CHATELARD

(*Outside*). But if my queen and lady note it—ah, what other advertisement would a man desire?
(MARY *the Queen enters with* CHATELARD, CHATELHERAULT, *and the* FOUR MARYS-IN-WAITING.)

MARY

Tut, if it were not known, or suspected, that I was queen, I should have stepped in bog like a drover's daughter——

CHATELARD

Madame, that you are queen would be known if the world were stripped of subjects. The very trees and frozen mountains would bow down to you!

MARY

(*Laughing*). I can well imagine.
Body o' me, I could wish the clouds would stoop less to their queen in my native land.

CHATELHERAULT

One forgets how damn dismal this Scotland can be.

MARY

Dismal? Traitor, have you never plucked a gowan in spring—a fairy fresh gowan—?

CHATELHERAULT

Late—it comes late here—

MARY

Or gorged with bright thorn-apples in mid-August?

CHATELHERAULT

Is there an August in this heathenish climate? God, I can't remember it!

MARY

They are sweeter here than in France, as I recall, and all fruits are sweeter here, of those that grow—and the summer's sweeter—

CHATELHERAULT

They're short enough, God knows.

THE OLD MAN

And when they come they will bring excellent devices of masks and ornament to deceive the eye, and soft words and stenches to cumber the senses of mankind. Adulterers, jig-masters and the like will come in authority, and their counsel will be whoring and carousing, the flower and fruits of evil, of that great sin, that sin that

eats at the heart of the world, the church
of abominations, the church of Rome.
(*He pauses.* MARY *stops to look back at
him.*)

MARY

Chatelherault, I have been long away, and
the speech of Scotland falls strangely on
my ears, but is this talk usual among my
people?

THE OLD MAN

Yet is there a place reserved for them,
where the fire is unending and abates not,
even as their desires abate not, where their
tender flesh shall be torn from them with
white-hot pincers, nor shall rank or station
avail them, whether they be queens or
kings or the lemans of queens and kings—!

MARY

(*Tremulous*). Surely this is some jest, sir.
Surely this is not said in welcome to me.

THE OLD MAN

And what other welcome shall we give the
whore of Babylon—the leprous and canker-
ous evangel of the Beast!
(BOTHWELL *returns from the right.*)

BOTHWELL

Your Majesty, they are preparing a room
at the inn, and the chair will be here at
once. If you would deign to take my cloak
for your shoulders—
(*He lays his cloak around her.*)

MARY

Thank you. I wish to speak to this gentleman—

BOTHWELL

This is Master John Knox, of whom your
Grace may have heard.

MARY

Nay, then I have heard of him, and I wish
to speak to him. Master Knox, it is true
that I am Mary Stuart, and your queen,
and I have come back from France after
many years away, to take up my rule in
this country. It is true, too, that I am sad
to leave the south and the sun, and I come

here knowing that I shall meet with diffi-
culties that would daunt many older and
wiser than I am—for I am young and inexperienced and perhaps none too adept in
statecraft. Yet this is my native place, Master Knox, and I loved it as a child and still
love it—and whatever I may lack in experi-
ence, whatever I may have too much of
youth, I shall try to make up for, if my
people will help me, in tolerance and
mercy, and a quick eye for wrongs and a
quick hand to right them—

THE OLD MAN

Aye, they told me you spoke honey—

MARY

And cannot you also—you and your people
and those you know—cannot you too be
tolerant toward me a little space while I
find my way? For it will be hard enough
at the friendliest.

THE OLD MAN

Woman, I remember whose daughter and
whose voice you are—

MARY

If I were your daughter, Master Knox, and
this task before me, would you think it
fitting to lay such hard terms on me, beast
and whore and I know not what? For I
am not a whore, I can say truly, but the
daughter of a prince, softly nurtured and
loving honor and truth. Neither is my body
corrupt, nor my mind. Nay, I am near to
tears that you should think so, and I was
not far from tears before, finding myself
unexpected on this coast, and no prepara-
tion to receive me. What you have said
comes as very cold comfort now when I
need greeting and reassurance.

BOTHWELL

Your Majesty, if the old goat has said any-
thing that needs retracting—

MARY

He shall retract nothing in fear! I would
have all men my friends in Scotland!

BOTHWELL

I'm afraid that's past praying for.

MARY

Look on me, sir—and judge my face and my words. In all fairness, am I the evangel of the Beast? Can we not be friends?

THE OLD MAN

I fear not, madame.

MARY

I strongly desire it. I have no wish for any enemy of mine except that he become my friend. You most of all, for I have met you first, and it is an augury.

THE OLD MAN

Your Majesty, I have said what I came to say.

MARY

But you no. longer mean it! See—I give you my hand, Master Knox—it is a queen's hand, and fair—and I look at you out of honest eyes—and I mean well and fairly—you cannot refuse me! Do you still hesitate? It is clean.
(*She smiles. He bows stiffly over her hand.*)
And will you come to see me at Holyroodhouse, and give me counsel? For God knows I shall need counsel—and I shall listen, that I promise.

THE OLD MAN

Your Majesty, I should be untrue to myself and my calling if I refused counsel where it is asked.

MARY

You will come?

THE OLD MAN

I will come.

MARY

I will send for you, and soon.
(*Her words are a kindly dismissal.*)

THE OLD MAN

Good night, Your Majesty—

MARY

Good night, Master Knox.
(KNOX *goes to the left.*)
Now I wonder, will he hate me more or less?

BOTHWELL

More, probably. However, it's just as well to have him where you can watch him.

MARY

You're an outspoken man yourself, Captain.

BOTHWELL

I am.

MARY

You will forgive me, but so far I have not heard your name.

CHATELHERAULT

The Captain is James Hepburn, madame —the Earl of Bothwell.

MARY

Ah—you fought ably for my mother.

BOTHWELL

I have been of some slight service here and there.

MARY

You have indeed! Tell me, my lord of Bothwell, have I done well so far? Shall I not make this Scotland mine?

BOTHWELL

Madame, it is a cold, dour, sour, bastardly villainous country, and the folk on it are a cold, dour, sour, bastardly lot of close-shaving psalm-retching villains, and I can only hope no harm will come here to that bonny face of yours, and no misery to the spirit you bring.

MARY

Now here's a new kind of courtesy!

BOTHWELL

You'll hear far and wide I'm no courtier, madame—but I have eyes, and I can see that the new sovereign is a sonsie lass and a keen one, and I was for her from the first I saw her face—but from my heart I could wish her a better country to rule over—

MARY

Now, will no one speak well of this poor Scotland of mine—?

BOTHWELL

Your Majesty, shall I praise it for you—as high as it deserves—?

MARY

Say whatever good you can!

BOTHWELL

Then this is Scotland, my lady: To the north a few beggarly thousands of Highland Catholics who have not yet learned the trick of wearing britches, and to the south a few beggarly thousands of Lowland Protestants whose britches have no pockets to them—Their pleasures are drinking and fighting, both of which they do badly, and what they fight about is that half of them are willing to sell their souls for a florin, whereas the other half has no expectation of getting so much. What business they have is buying cheap and selling dear, but since none of them will sell cheap, and none will pay dear, the upshot is there's no business done——

MARY

Enough, enough!—solemnly and truly, sir —it may be they are not a happy race, but they have beliefs—and what they believe they believe from the heart! Even this Master Knox—

BOTHWELL

He? He believes whatever's to his own advantage, and prophesies whatever will line his nest if it comes to pass. He makes his living yelling nonsense into the lugs of these poor, benighted, superstitious savages —he's split the country wide open over your coming and leads the pack against you, brawling from his dung-hill! We'll have blood-shed over it yet—

MARY

Blood-shed?

BOTHWELL

And plenty.

MARY

No. If I thought that I should turn now and bid the mariners hoist sail and put

back for France. I shall win, but I shall win in a woman's way, not by the sword.

BOTHWELL

Let us hope so.

MARY

Hope so! But I shall!

BOTHWELL

I am no courtier, madame. I say, let us hope so.

MARY BEATON

The chair has come, madame.

MARY

Yes, and in time. We're chilled to the heart here. Come.

(*She goes out with* BOTHWELL, *the others following. The first and third* GUARDS *return.*)

FIRST GUARD

Did the old man spit his venom?

SECOND GUARD

You'll not believe it. He kissed her hand.

THIRD GUARD

She's a witch, then.

SECOND GUARD

Aye, is she. The kind a man wouldna mind being bewitched by.

THIRD GUARD

No.

SECOND GUARD

I tell you she fair wenched him. The old man doddert a bit and then bent over like a popinjay.

FIRST GUARD

She's tha' kind then?

SECOND GUARD

She's tha' kind.

Curtain

SCENE II

SCENE: *A corner of Queen Elizabeth's study at Whitehall. It is morning, but the sun has not yet risen. She is up early to go over plans with* LORD BURGHLEY, *who sits opposite her at a small table on which an hour-glass stands like a paper-weight on their notes. She is a young woman, still beautiful, with a crafty face. Tall candles burn behind them in a sconce. Outside the circle of light the scene is indefinite.*

BURGHLEY

It still lacks something of dawn, Your Majesty.

ELIZABETH

We have one more hour before the palace will be stirring. You said, I believe, that you have made memoranda in regard to Mary Stuart?

BURGHLEY

I have set down the facts as we must face them, and alternative policies.

ELIZABETH

Read them, if you will. And turn the glass. It's run out.

BURGHLEY

(*Turning the glass and taking up a paper*). They are not in order, but the main points are covered. First, Mary Stuart has crossed from France to Scotland against your advice and without your safe conduct. This is in itself a slight to Your Majesty, and almost a challenge, though not one of which you can take public cognizance.

ELIZABETH

Yes.

BURGHLEY

Second, she has been crowned queen of Scotland, this also against your wish and in defiance of your policy. This may be construed as an open breach of friendship, or may be overlooked, as Your Majesty may desire—and as it may seem best.

ELIZABETH

Yes.

BURGHLEY

Third, she is a Catholic and related by blood to the most powerful Catholic house in France, which constitutes her a public

danger to Protestant England. Fourth, she is next heir after Your Majesty to the throne of England, and is held by Catholic Europe to be the rightful queen of England at the present time, Your Majesty being regarded by all Catholics as a pretender, unjustly seated on your throne.

ELIZABETH

True. Proceed. You have more on that point. They believe me a bastard and say so. Very well, let us face that, too.

BURGHLEY

Fifth, then—you are held by the Catholic Europe to be the illegitimate daughter of Henry the Eighth, the divorce of Henry from Catherine of Arragon being unrecognized by the Church of Rome and his marriage to your mother, Anne Boleyn, deemed invalid. Sixth, these things being true, Your Majesty must not allow Mary Stuart to succeed as Queen of Scotland. For in so far as she is secure in Scotland you are insecure in England. Your Majesty will forgive my bad habit of setting down in writing what is so obvious, but it is only by looking hard at these premises that I am able to discover what must be done.

ELIZABETH

Out with it then. What must be done?

BURGHLEY

She must be defeated.

ELIZABETH

How?

BURGHLEY

Is there more than one way? We must pick our quarrel and send an army into Scotland.

ELIZABETH

Declare war?

BURGHLEY

Perhaps not openly—but we have excuse for it.

ELIZABETH

And reason?

BURGHLEY

She must be defeated.

ELIZABETH

Truly, but not so quick, not so quick with wars and troops and expenses. Have you no better counsel?

BURGHLEY

In all my reading I have found no case of a sovereign deposed without violence.

ELIZABETH

And in all those voluminous notes of yours you have set down no other method save warfare? The last resort, the most difficult, costly and hazardous of all?

BURGHLEY

It is the only sure method, and you cannot afford to fail.

ELIZABETH

My dear Burghley, in any project which affects England and our own person so nearly we have no intention of failing. But you have overlooked in your summary two considerations which simplify the problem. One is the internal dissension in Scotland, half Protestant, half Catholic, and divided in a mortal enmity—

BURGHLEY

Overlooked it! Madame, it is the main argument for an immediate declaration of war—Edinburgh would rally to your arms overnight! This is our opportunity to unite England and Scotland!

ELIZABETH

A war would unite Scotland against us— unite Scotland under Mary. No—it is necessary first to undermine her with her own subjects.

BURGHLEY

And how would that be accomplished?

ELIZABETH

This brings me to the second consideration which you overlook—the conduct and reputation of Mary herself.

BURGHLEY

Would that affect our policy?

ELIZABETH

It will make it. Merely to remind us, will you read over again the report of Mary's character in Randolph's latest budget of news?

BURGHLEY

This? "As for the person of Marie, our new Queen, I must say in truth that she is of high carriage, beautiful in a grave way—?"

ELIZABETH

So—go on.

BURGHLEY

"Beautiful, in a grave way, somewhat gamesome and given to lightness of manner among her lords as well as with other company, very quick-witted to answer back, and addicted to mirth and dancing, wherewith she hath made many converts to her cause among those most disaffected, though there be also those found to say her manners might more beseem the stews or places of low resort than so ancient a palace and line—"

ELIZABETH

You see, she is a Stuart.

BURGHLEY

"Moreover, she hath allowed herself to be seen much in the company of certain men, among them the Earl of Bothwell, and hath borne herself among these men, they being known of somewhat loose report, in such fashion as to give scandal to the stricter sort here, she not scanting to lend her eyes or hands or tongue to a kind of nimble and facile exchange of smiles and greetings which might better become the hostess of an ale-house, seeking to win custom. Natheless she is liked, and greatly liked by those on whom she hath smiled closely, they being won not as a wise sovereign wins subjects, but as a woman wins men."

ELIZABETH

Yes, a Stuart.

BURGHLEY

"Yet to be true again I must say also that she is of noble mind, greatly religious in her way, and the whispers against her name not justified by what she is in herself, but only by her manners, which she hath brought from France."

ELIZABETH

She has won our Randolph among others. He shall go north no more.

BURGHLEY

"And in addition she hath borne her power thus far with so discreet and tolerant a justness, impartial to north and south, to Catholic and Protestant alike, that if she persevere in this fashion she is like to reconcile the factions and establish herself firmly on the throne of Scotland. For vast numbers who thought to curse her now remain her fast friends."

ELIZABETH

Have you yet seen what we must do?

BURGHLEY

I find in this only a graver and more malicious danger.

ELIZABETH

And you would still make war?

BURGHLEY

Your Majesty, it will be war whether we like it or not—and there is imminent danger, danger to your throne and life. The more suddenly you act the less effort will be needed—

ELIZABETH

My lord, my lord, it is hard to thrust a queen from her throne, but suppose a

queen were led to destroy herself, led carefully from one step to another in a long descent until at last she stood condemned among her own subjects, barren of royalty, stripped of force, and the people of Scotland were to deal with her for us?

BURGHLEY

She would crush a rebellion.

ELIZABETH

She would now, but wait. She is a Catholic, and for that half her people distrust her. She has a name for coquetry and easy smiling, and we shall build that up into a name for wantonness and loose behavior. She is seen to have French manners; we shall make it appear that these manners indicate a false heart and hollow faith.

BURGHLEY

Can this be done?

ELIZABETH

She is a woman, remember, and open to attack as a woman. We shall set tongues wagging about her. And since it may be true that she is of a keen and noble mind, let us take care of that too. Let us marry her to a weakling and a fool. A woman's mind and spirit are no better than those of the man she lies under in the night.

BURGHLEY

She will hardly marry to our convenience, madame.

ELIZABETH

Not if she were aware of it. But she is next heir to my throne; she will hope for children to sit on it, and she will therefore wish to marry a man acceptable as the father of kings. We can make use of that.

BURGHLEY

Only perhaps.

ELIZABETH

No, certainly. She is a woman and already jealous for the children she may bear. To my mind the man she marries must be of good appearance, in order that she may want him, but a fool, in order that he may ruin her, and a Catholic, in order to set half her people against her.

BURGHLEY

We know that she is seen much with Bothwell.

ELIZABETH

And he is a Protestant.

BURGHLEY

He is a Protestant. Now suddenly it occurs to me. If she were to marry a Protestant and turn Protestant herself, would she not make an acceptable ally?——

ELIZABETH

(*Rising*). I do not wish her for an ally! Have you not yet understood? I wish her a Catholic and an enemy, that I may see her blood run at my feet! Since Bothwell is a Protestant, the more reason for dangling some handsome youngster instantly in the north, as if by accident, nay, as if against my will, some youngster with courtly manners, lacking in brain, a Catholic, and of a blood-strain that would strengthen pretensions to the throne of England.

BURGHLEY

You have thought of some one?

ELIZABETH

I have thought of several. I shall even let it be rumored that I oppose such a marriage. I shall let it go abroad that I favor some one else.

BURGHLEY

Who is the man?

ELIZABETH

I have thought of Darnley.

BURGHLEY

But after herself Darnley is in fact heir to the English throne. An alliance with him would actually strengthen her claim to succeed to your place.

ELIZABETH

The better, the better. He is handsome, and of good bearing?

BURGHLEY

Yes.

ELIZABETH

And a fool?

BURGHLEY

A boasting, drunken boy.

ELIZABETH

And a Catholic.

BURGHLEY

As you know.

ELIZABETH

If I give out that I am determined against it, she will marry him, and he will drag her down, awaken her senses to become his slave, turn her people against her, make her a fool in council, curb this pretty strumpetry that gains her friends, haul her by the hair for jealousy, get her big with child, too, and spoil her beauty. I tell you a queen who marries is no queen, a woman who marries is a puppet—and she will marry—she must marry to staunch that Stuart blood.

BURGHLEY

This will take time.

ELIZABETH

It may take many years. I can wait.

BURGHLEY

And we shall need many devices.

ELIZABETH

You shall not find me lacking in devices, in the word to drop here, the rumor started there. We must have constant knowledge of her, and agents about her continually, so that her acts and sayings may be misconstrued and a net of half-lies woven about her, yes, till her people believe her a voluptuary, a scavenger of dirty loves, a bedder with grooms. Aye, till she herself think ill of herself and question her loves, lying awake in torment in the dark.— There is a man called Knox who can be used in this.

BURGHLEY

But that—to accomplish that—

ELIZABETH

We live in a world of shadows, my lord; we are not what we are, but what is said of us and what we read in others' eyes. More especially is this true of queens and kings. It will grow up about her in whispers that she is tainted in blood, given over to lechery and infamous pleasures. She will be known as double-tongued, a demon with an angel's face, insatiable in desire, an emissary of Rome, a prophetess of evil addicted to lascivious rites and poisonous revenges. And before all this her own mind will pause in doubt and terror of what she may be that these things should be said of her—she will lie awake in torment in the dark—and she will lie broken, nerveless there in the dark. Her own people will rise and take her sceptre from her.

BURGHLEY

(*Rising*). But Your Majesty—you—

ELIZABETH

However, I am not to appear in this. Always, and above all, I am to seem her friend.—You would say that I am in myself more nearly what will be said of her.

BURGHLEY

No, no—

ELIZABETH

Why, perhaps. But that is not what is said of me. Whatever I may be, it shall be said only that I am the queen of England, and that I rule well.

Curtain

SCENE III

SCENE: *A great hall in Mary Stuart's apartments at Holyroodhouse. The room is rectangular, with wide fireplaces glowing to the left and right. An entrance door opens to the right, and two doors at the left lead, one to Mary's study, and the other to her bedroom. The stone of the walls is largely covered with stamped leather hangings. A chair, slightly elevated, stands in the middle of the rear wall, the royal arms of Scotland draped above it. The floor is stone with a few Eastern rugs. There are two high, heavily draped windows at the rear, on either side of the queen's chair.*

MARY BEATON, MARY SETON, *and* MARY LIVINGSTONE *are concerning themselves with the hanging of the ensign behind the chair, and* LIVINGSTONE *has stepped upon a stool to reach a fold of it.* LORD DARNLEY *and* LORD GORDON *are warming themselves at one of the fires, having just come in.*

BEATON

(*To the men*). It's to hang there because she wants it there. Isn't that enough?

GORDON

I've heard my father say that the kings of Scotland were always plain folk, but queens are a fancy breed, and their ways are fancy.

DARNLEY

A thought higher with that fold, my dear —just a thought higher.

LIVINGSTONE

(*Turning*). And why?

DARNLEY

Dod, lady, it's a neat turn of ankle you show when you reach up. Reach a bit higher.

LIVINGSTONE

(*Back to her work*). Look your eyes full if it does you any good, my Lord Darnley.

DARNLEY

Man, man, but that's a pretty foot!

GORDON

Aye.

DARNLEY

Ye have heard it said, no doubt, what they say about a woman's foot?

GORDON

Aye.

SETON

What do they say?

DARNLEY

About a woman's foot? Only that it's, in a sort, a measure of her capacities.

BEATON

Oh, is it, indeed? I've heard the same in respect to a man's nose, and I can only say if it's true your nose is no great advertisement for you.

DARNLEY

The nose is a fallible signal, my lady, as I'll prove to you—you naming your own place and time.

BEATON

I to name the place?

DARNLEY

It is your privilege.

BEATON

Your own bed-chamber, then.

LIVINGSTONE

Beaton!

DARNLEY

Accepted! Accepted! My own bed-chamber! And the time?

BEATON

The night of your wedding, by God!

DARNLEY

My dear lady—

GORDON

She has you there, Darnley.

BEATON

Moreover, if there is one kind of man a woman dislikes more than another it's one so little experienced that he goes peeping at ankles for lack of better satisfaction.

DARNLEY

Stop there! I will furnish you with data—

BEATON

Unless indeed it be the kind of man whose experiences with women have been like nothing so much as those of a dog with lamp-posts—

LIVINGSTONE

Beaton!

(MARY FLEMING *enters from the queen's study.*)

BEATON

(*Clapping a hand to her mouth in mock chagrin*). Oh, what have I said, what have I said?

SETON

A great plenty!

DARNLEY

Mistress Fleming, is it true our sovereign is inaccessible this day?

FLEMING

Quite true, I fear.

DARNLEY

God help the man who tries to woo a queen.

FLEMING

And so he might if your Lordship prayed to him with any serious intent.

DARNLEY

Perhaps. And yet I doubt it might do more good if a man were to have studied in France.

FLEMING

Studied?

DARNLEY

The arts. The arts of Ovid. The arts of pleasing a maid.

BEATON

They are the same in France as elsewhere, no doubt.

DARNLEY

No doubt, says she, and a very pretty innocence.

GORDON

Aye, as though she'd never been there.

FLEMING

We're not denying that we've been in France.

DARNLEY

Then don't tell us that the art of Love is the same there as in England and Scotland, for the report runs different.

GORDON

It's a kennt thing that French love is none the same.

LIVINGSTONE

Will you tell us how?

GORDON

Eh, we're to tell you who've lived among them?

FLEMING

Aside from better manners the people of France are like the people of Scotland, both in love and war.

DARNLEY

It's not an easy matter to go into with my lady's bevy of beauty, nevertheless they say there are no virgins there above four years old.

LIVINGSTONE

Then they lie who say it, and you're fools to believe it.

DARNLEY

Nay, it may be a bit exaggerated, but I'd lay no more than a groat on any piece of French virginity. They have summat to tell in confession; they have had their three of a night; they have had their what-for, and come up all the fresher and more lisping for it.

BEATON

I must say I've never met nastier minds than hereabout, and that's something for John Knox to ponder on, too.

GORDON

Will ye come, man? Ye'll have no sight of the queen today, and these trollops have no time for plain Scotchmen.

DARNLEY

Aye.

FLEMING

Lord Darnley is to remain within call. It is her Majesty's pleasure.

DARNLEY

Ah, well that's something.

GORDON

It's dangling, to give it a plain name. (BOTHWELL *enters from the right.*)

LIVINGSTONE

Oh, my lord Bothwell.

BOTHWELL

By God, my name's remembered, and that's a triumph,
Tell the sweet queen Lord Bothwell would see her alone.

LIVINGSTONE

Sir, she is closeted with her secretary—
We are not free to speak with her.

BOTHWELL

Closeted? So?
I like not that word closeted. Who is there here
Who can speak with her and tell her?

FLEMING

My Lord, she has spaced
This day off into hours, so many to each,
And I fear your name is not scheduled.

BOTHWELL

Distrust your schedule,
Then, my prim, for I'll see her.

FLEMING

The ambassador

From England arrives today, for his audi-
ence,
And before that Her Majesty plans to hold
A conclave with the lords.

DARNLEY

We've been sloughed off
Much the same way, my lord.

BOTHWELL

Run along then, and practise
Wearing that tin sword you've got hung
on you,
Before it trips you.

DARNLEY

Trips me?

BOTHWELL

Aye, run and play!
This one's been used. The nicks along the
edge
Were made on tougher than you. Tell my
lady queen
I wish to see her now.

FLEMING

I cannot myself.
I might speak to Master Rizzio.

BOTHWELL

Then do that. Is Scotland grown so formal
That a man's received like a money-
lender?
(FLEMING goes out.)

LIVINGSTONE

No,
But these matters must be arranged.

BOTHWELL

(To DARNLEY). Are you still here?

DARNLEY

Still here.

BOTHWELL

I knew a pimp in Paris had much your
look,
But the women he brought me were foul.

DARNLEY

But good enough,
I daresay.

BOTHWELL

You might have thought so.
(RIZZIO enters. FLEMING following.)

RIZZIO

Oh, my lord Bothwell,
There's such great pressure on our time
today—
Matters that must be seen to; if you could
come
Tomorrow—

BOTHWELL

Well, I cannot come tomorrow.
Tomorrow will not do. I am here today.
And will not be here tomorrow. Is that
understood?
(RIZZIO pauses.)

DARNLEY

Let him run his suit into the ground.

GORDON

Aye, and himself.
(DARNLEY and GORDON go out.)

RIZZIO

My orders are strict, my lord. Her Majesty
Has great problems of state—

BOTHWELL

And they concern me
More than some others. Now, before
Christ, I've argued
Enough with women and women-faced
men! A room's a room
And a door's a door! Shall I enter without
warning
Or will you announce me to her? Great
pressure on
Our time! Our time, he says! My fine
Italian—
(MARY STUART enters. There is sudden
quiet.)

MARY

I will speak with my lord alone.
(One by one, and silently, RIZZIO and the
girls go out.)
Do I find you angry?

BOTHWELL

At these pests and midges.

MARY

You saw me yesterday.

BOTHWELL

I have been standing since this early morn-
ing—
I and some hundred crows, out in the
coppice
On the cliff's edge, waiting for the smoke
to rise
From your breakfast chimney. And by the
Lord these crows
Are a funny company. I've had four full
hours
To study them.

MARY

You come to tell me this?

BOTHWELL

I come to tell you
I've never shown such patience for a wo-
man,
Not in my life before.

MARY

Did you call it patience
On a time when I could not see you, to
wreck an inn,
Leave mine host in the road with a broken
head
And lie with his daughter?

BOTHWELL

That was not true. Or at least
I had her good will for it.

MARY

And another time
To besiege the governor's house with your
border knaves
And rouse all Edinburgh? Are you a man
Or a storm at sea, not to be brought in-
doors?

BOTHWELL

When I would see my girl, why I must
see her
Or I am a storm, and indoors, too.

MARY

Your girl? Give me leave,
Since I am a queen, with a kingdom to
reign over,
To queen it once in a while.

BOTHWELL

I tell you truly
I've the manners of a rook, for we're all
crows here,
And that's what's understood in this town,
but I could
Be tame and split my tongue with courtly
speeches
If I could be sure of you—if I could know
from one day
To another what to make of your ways
You shut yourself up
With secretaries and ministers, harking for
weeks
On end to their truffle—while I perch me
on the rocks
And look my eyes out.

MARY

When I was but thirteen
A pretty lad fell in love with me; he'd
come,
Oh, afternoons, late midnight, early dawn
Sopping with dew-fall; he'd stand there,
waiting for a glance—
I've never had such tribute.

BOTHWELL

This is no boy.
This is a man comes beating your door in
now.
It may be you're too young to know the
difference,
But it's time you learned.

MARY

You've had your way, my lord;
We've spoken together, though I had no
time to give,
And now, with your pardon—

BOTHWELL

You'll go about the business
Of marrying some one else. That's what
this mangy
Meeting of councillors means, and that's
what portends
From Elizabeth's ambassador! I warn you,
Make no decisions without me!

MARY

I cannot marry you.
I beg you, ask it not; speak not of it. Our
day
Has come between us. Let me go now.

BOTHWELL

My lady,
I will speak softly. Have no fear of me
Or what I intend. But there have been days
I remember
When you had less care what hostages you
gave
The world. I think you showed more
royally then
Than now, for you loved then and spoke
your love, and I
Moved more than mortal for that while.
Oh, girl,
If we would be as the high gods, we must
live
From within outward! Let the heavens
rain fire
Or the earth mud. This is a muddy race
That breeds around us. Will you walk in
fear of mud-slingers,
Or walk proudly, and take my hand?

MARY

I am a queen.

BOTHWELL

They've made a slave of you,
This bastard half-brother of yours, this fox
of a Maitland,
This doddering Chatelherault! They
frighten you
With consequences. They're afraid of
men's tongues
And they've made you afraid. But what
they truly fear
Is that you'll win the country, be queen
here truly
And they'll be out of it. What they'd like
best of all
Is to wreck you, break you completely, rule
the country themselves,
And why they fear me is because I'm your
man alone,
And man enough to stop them.

MARY

Yes. You are man enough.
It's dangerous to be honest with you, my
Bothwell,
But honest I'll be. Since I've been woman
grown
There's been no man save you but I could
take
His hand steadily in mine, and look in his
eyes

Steadily, too, and feel in myself more
power
Than I felt in him. All but yourself. There
is aching
Fire between us, fire that could take deep
hold
And burn down all the marches of the west
And make us great or slay us. Yet it's not
to be trusted.
Our minds are not the same. If I gave my
hand
To you, I should be pledged to rule by
wrath
And violence, to take without denial,
And mount on others' ruin. That's your
way
And it's not mine.

BOTHWELL

You'll find no better way.
There's no other way for this nation of
churls and cravens.

MARY

I have been queen of France—a child-
queen and foolish—
But one thing I did learn, that to rule
gently
Is to rule wisely. The knives you turn on
your people
You must some time take in your breast.

BOTHWELL

You know not Scotland.
Here you strike first or die. Your brother
Moray
Seeks your death, Elizabeth of England
Seeks your death, and they work together.

MARY

Nay—
You mistrust too much—and even if this
were true
A sovereign lives always with death before
and after,
And many have tried to murder their way
to safety—
But there's no safety there. For each enemy
You kill, you make ten thousand, for each
one
You spare, you make one friend.

BOTHWELL

Friends? Friends? Oh, lass,
Thou'lt nurse these adders and they'll fang
thee—Thou'rt

Too tender and too just. My heart cries for
thee—
Take my help, take my hands!

MARY

I would I could take both.
God knows how I wish it. But as I am
queen
My heart shall not betray me, what I be-
lieve
And my faith. This is my faith, dear my
lord, that all men
Love better good than evil, cling rather to
truth
Than falseness, answer fair dealing with
fair return;
And this too; those thrones will fall that
are built on blood
And craft, that as you'd rule long, you
must rule well.—
This has been true, and is true.

BOTHWELL

God help thee, child.

MARY

Be staunch to me. You have been staunch-
est of all.
Let me not lose your arm. No, nor your
love—
You know how much you have of mine.
I'm here
Alone, made queen in a set, hard, bitter
time.
Aid me, and not hinder.

BOTHWELL

So it shall be.

MARY

And give me the help I'd have.

BOTHWELL

That I can't promise.
I'll help thee and defend thee. Lady dear,
Do you use guile on me?

MARY

No, sweet, I love thee.
And I could love thee well.
(*She goes to him. He kisses her hand and
then her lips.*)
Go now, and leave me.
We've been seen too much together.

BOTHWELL

You must lay this hand
In no one's else. It's mine.

MARY

I have but lease on it,
Myself. It's not my own. But it would be
yours
If it were mine to give.
(*MARY LIVINGSTONE comes to the right-
hand door.*)

LIVINGSTONE

Your Majesty,
The Lords of the council are here.

MARY

Let them be admitted.
(*LIVINGSTONE goes out.*)

BOTHWELL

Has Your Majesty forgotten
That I am of the council, under your seal?

MARY

I could wish you were elsewhere. These are
the men I least
Have wanted to find us alone. But stay,
now you're here.
(*She goes pensively to her chair of state
and seats herself.* LORD JAMES STUART, *Earl
of Moray,* MAITLAND OF LETHINGTON, *the*
DUC DE CHATELHERAULT, HUNTLEY, MOR-
TON, *and* ERSKINE *are ushered in by* MARY
LIVINGSTONE, *who withdraws. There is a
brief silence.*)

MAITLAND

We have not interrupted Your Majesty?

MARY

No. The Earl of Bothwell is of the council.
I have asked him to take part.

MAITLAND

There was some agreement
That since the Earl's name might come up,
it would be as well
If he were not here.

BOTHWELL

And then again, since my name
May be mentioned, and there's none so
able as I

To defend it, it may be as well that I'm
here.

MAITLAND

My lord,
There was small thought to attack you.

BOTHWELL

Less now, perhaps.

MARY

Lord Bothwell will remain.

MORAY

Sister, it may be that Bothwell will be
offended
By something said.

MARY

You are courtier enough,
To couch it not to offend, my brother.

MAITLAND

Nay then,
What we have come to say must be softly
said,
But meant no less strictly. The question of
our queen's marriage,
Of which every one has spoken, let me add,
But which we have avoided here, must
now come up
Whether or no we like it.

MARY

Be not so tender
With me, dear Maitland. I have been mar-
ried. I am
A widow, and free to marry again.

HUNTLEY

That's the lass!
They say widows are always ready.

MARY

Do they say that?
Do they not say ready but—wary?

HUNTLEY

Aye, that too.

MARY

But the truth is I should prefer my own
time for wedding.
I know of no prince or king whose hand
is offered,
And whose hand I'd take.

MAITLAND

It's not to be treated lightly
I'm much afraid. The thrones of all the
world
Are shaken with broils even as we stand
here. The throne
On which you sit, our sovereign, is shaken,
too,
Though Your Majesty has done more than
I'd have dreamed
Could be done to still the factions. It's our
belief
That a marriage, if the right one, would
seat you more firmly,
Put an end to many questions.

MARY

There's more of this?

MAITLAND

That's all we wish—to see you safe on your
throne
So that we may be safe in our houses. Until
men know
What alliance we're to make, what hangs
over us
In the way of foreign treaties, the clans will
sleep
With dirks in their brogans, and a weather
eye still open
For fire in the thatch. And yet to choose
the man—
That's a point we can't agree on.

MARY

I'm with you there.
For you see, I'm hard to please.

MAITLAND

And more than that,
Of princes that offer, or have been sug-
gested, each one
Commits us to some alliance of church or
state
We'd find embarrassing. Philip of Spain,
the Duke
Of Anjou—these are Catholic—

BOTHWELL

Has it crossed your mind
That there are lords in Scotland?

MAITLAND

And there, too—
If the choice were to fall on a Scottish earl,
the houses

Passed over would take it ill—and it might
  well lead
To a breach in our peace—

BOTHWELL

Yes?

MAITLAND

Nay, even to civil war.

MARY

I cannot give myself out
As a virgin queen, yet our cousin Eliza-
  beth's plan
Has virtues. Must I marry at all?

MORTON

Your Majesty,
We have not yet said what we came to say,
And it needs saying bluntly. The people of
  Scotland
Are given to morals almost as much as to
  drink.
I'll not say they're moral themselves, but
  they'll insist
On morals in high places. And they've got
  in their heads
That you're a light woman.
(MARY RISES.)
I don't know how it got there,
And I daresay it's not true—

MARY

Thank you. For your daresay.

MAITLAND

I could have wished to speak more deli-
  cately
Of this, but it's before us, and can't be
  denied.
Your Majesty, when you came to us from
  France
And I saw you first, I said to myself in my
  heart,
All will be well with Scotland. What I
  thought then
I can say now, for you are wiser even
Than I had supposed, and you have dealt
  more justly
Than any could have hoped, yet still it's
  true
Some spreading evil has gone out against
  you,
A crawling fog of whispers.

MARY

Who believes them?

MAITLAND

I'll not say they're believed. I'm not sure
  they are.
But there was the episode of the boy who
  was hidden
In your bed-chamber—

ERSKINE

Chatelard.

MAITLAND

Aye, he, and
That may have begun it. I believed at first
  it stemmed
From John Knox's preaching, for he holds
  all Catholics
To be the devil's own, but there's more
  than that—
A much more seeded, intentional crop of
  lyings
Planted here, till I've wondered if Chatelard
May not have been an agent, or one of
  many.

MARY

Planted by whom?

HUNTLEY

Why, by Elizabeth.
Who else?

MAITLAND

But that's not certain, either.
Chatelard came from France, and in all
  this scurril
I've traced no word to London.

MARY

It's what they say.
Not what they believe.

HUNTLEY

You've lent them some color for it,
Your Majesty. You've been no statue.

MARY

No,
Nor wish to be. My Lord of Lethington,
What you have said to me, how I was
  when you saw me,

How I seem to you now, I swear to you,
you were not wrong.
I have not betrayed myself as woman or
queen.

MAITLAND

I would swear that, too.

MARY

And since I know that is true,
I have thought very little of whispers. For
there is judgment
Somehow in the air; what I am will be
known, what's false
Will wash out in the rains.
(*She seats herself again.*)

MAITLAND

My sovereign, you are yet young.
I once believed that. But I have lived long
enough
To see error grow up and prosper, and
send its roots
A century deep. There's force enough in
these winds
Of malice to blow us all down—

MARY

I'll try to be serious,
For I see you are. It's your thought, then,
that a marriage
Would end the rumors?

MAITLAND

Aye.

MARY

But as to whom I'll marry—
Happily, that's not decided for me yet.

MORTON

By God,
If it was we'd see you to bed with him
tonight.

MARY

Has the woman no voice in such matters?

MORTON

Not in such cases.

MARY

And what is my case, may I ask?

MORTON

Why, we've said nothing
About my Lord Bothwell. It's his name's
coupled with yours;
His and young Rizzio's.

BOTHWELL

I've thought often, Morton.
One of us would die before the other. Now
I'm sure of it. And soon.

MORTON

I have you.

MARY

My lords,
Will you quarrel in council over your
queen's virtue?
Let me defend my own honor, and let you
Defend your own. Do I understand that I
Am accused with Bothwell or Rizzio? Or
both?

MAITLAND

You are accused of nothing.

MORTON

You are not accused,
Your Majesty. Moreover, you are queen
Of Scotland, and therefore no man here
would dare
Accuse you—

MARY

Oh, speak out, man! Are you afraid?
When have I punished plain dealing?

MORTON

Why, then, you are queen,
And may set your own customs, but if my
wife were seen
Abroad as you are, and half so free of con-
tact
With young and old as you are, I'd not
answer
For what was said about her!

MARY

I'm no man's wife.

MORTON

No. And the sense of this council
Is that it might be better if you were,
Better for your good name and better for
Scotland.

MARY

I will answer these things: as for Rizzio,
He is my secretary; if I spend time
In private with him, that is the reason. If I
Had not liked him, he would not be my
    secretary.
As for Lord Bothwell, he has put more
    strength
Behind what I wished to do than any
    among you,
And at times when I had despaired. He is
    my good friend.
We were here alone before this conference
And we differed in opinion. To wipe that
    out
I went to him of myself and kissed his lips.
We had kissed but once before, may not
    kiss again,
But that's at my option, not yours.

HUNTLEY

Lassie, ye've been
Too honest for your own good.

MARY

Why, if so much weight
Is placed on a kiss in Scotland, come now,
    each one
And take your kiss—or if that's no recom-
    pense
Come to me then in private, and you shall
    have,
Each one, one kiss.

MORTON

And after that, there are kisses
Elsewhere—and when you've finished,
    whether you'll marry
Or not may not be the question, but
    whether we can find
A prince who'll have you.

MARY

(*Rising and taking a step down*).
And having heard that word—
My lords, when you wish to talk with me
    again
As civilized men, and not barbarians,
You shall have audience. This Scottish kirk
    of yours
Has misled you as to the meaning of kisses.
    I am
Unsullied and young, and have my own
    faith to plight

And more to think of than these maunder-
    ings
Over pantry gossip. I shall not marry till
I find it wise, nor until I have made quite
    sure
What effect it will have on my inheritance
Of the throne of England. You come here
    in high conclave
And spend three farthing's worth of wit to
    chaffer
Over a kiss in my audience-chamber! The
    question
Is not to save my name, I hope, nor my
    throne,
But how best to meet the destiny that has
    made me
Full heir to all this island.—Scotland is
    mine,
And England will come to me or to the
    child
I hope to have. It's this that makes my mar-
    riage
A matter of moment.—And this—with
    your good pardon—
Will be the last for today.
(*She goes into her study.*)

MORAY

Morton, I warned you
To leave all speech to Lethington.

MORTON

She sits on that throne
Only so long as we want her there, no
    longer.

BOTHWELL

If my lord of Morton
Would care to lose those black feathers
    from his crest
I await his pleasure.
(*He goes out.*)

MORAY

I'm for that, too. Settle it between you,
And may you both win. We'll all be the
    better for it.
(LIVINGSTONE *enters from the right.*)

LIVINGSTONE

Lord Throgmorton is here from England
With embassies for the queen.

MAITLAND

She's gone to her study.
She'll wish to admit him.

LIVINGSTONE

Yes.
(*She goes to the queen's study.* MORTON *goes out the other door.*)

MAITLAND

We get no further
Today, then.
(*He goes to the door.*)

HUNTLEY

No. Erskine, a word with you.
(ERSKINE *and* HUNTLEY *go out.* THROGMORTON *enters.*)

MAITLAND

Come in, Lord Throgmorton. You've been
announced within.

THROGMORTON

Greetings, my lord, fair greetings.

MAITLAND

We can have speech later.

THROGMORTON

We shall.
(MAITLAND *goes out.* THROGMORTON *and* MORAY *are alone.*)
Greetings also to my Lord James Stuart,
In fine, the best of greetings.

MORAY

From Elizabeth?

THROGMORTON

I'm burdened with them—and more to you
than any.

MORAY

May I know the drift?

THROGMORTON

This is hardly the place for that,
But this much for now: Elizabeth has de-
termined
That you are to reign in Scotland, if not
as king,
Then as regent again.

MORAY

Well, that's news.

THROGMORTON

She bids me to tell you
As if from herself, you are not to be dis-
turbed
If her policy seems at variance with her
mind.
It's a wide arc of intrigue, but she carries
These schemes in her head like a gambit,
and she means
To play it to the end. Your sister Mary
Is not acceptable to her.

MORAY

But this scheme of hers?

THROGMORTON

Later, later. You're a silent man, I know.
No word.

MORAY

None.
(MARY *enters.*)

MARY

Lord Throgmorton?

THROGMORTON

Your Majesty.
(*He kneels. She comes to him and gives
him her hand to kiss.*)
From one great queen to another, happiness.

MARY

A courtier in the grand style.

THROGMORTON

Nay, Majesty,
A plain man of business.

MARY

Let us to business, then.
(*She motions him to rise, and he does so.*)
My brother, did you wish further word
with me?

MORAY

No, madame, only that I may see you tomorrow.

MARY

(*Goes to her chair*).
At your own time.

(MORAY *bows low and goes out.*)
You had more to say?

THROGMORTON

Much more. My poor brain's taxed with
remembering.
But to begin, Queen Elizabeth sends her
love
To her cousin of Scotland, wishes her well,
and a reign
Both long and easy, and proffers to that
end
Whatever friendship and amity between
thrones
Your Majesty will accept.

MARY

Tell Elizabeth
She will not find me niggard of friendship
or love.

THROGMORTON

I shall report Your Majesty so. Then, fur-
ther,
I'm bid to say, what Elizabeth most desires
Is that all briars of discord that have grown
Between this city and England, be wed
away,
And leave a path for peace.

MARY

I desire that, too.
Does she put a name to these briars?

THROGMORTON

Your Majesty, I am
Permitted to speak quite frankly?

MARY

I beg you to.

THROGMORTON

You are next heir to the throne of England,
and you
Are a Catholic. This is a danger to you
As well as Elizabeth. Were you to turn
Protestant
Elizabeth would at once recognize in you
Next heir to her succession.

MARY

I should think she might,
Since I am next heir.

THROGMORTON

Forgive me for speaking plainly.

MARY

Oh, forgive me!

THROGMORTON

If this seems difficult, I am bid to remind
you
That Elizabeth was a Catholic, but became
A Protestant for political reasons.

MARY

That
I could never do. Nor do I see that one's
faith
Should be touched by politics.

THROGMORTON

Why, not politics,
My gracious queen! God forbid me that I
should bring
That word into such a context! We know,
of course,
How one clings, shall we say for senti-
mental reasons,
To the rituals of his youth! Aye, and even
a prince,
We admit, would rather say his pater
nosters
The way he learned them when he was a
child. And yet
Must we take these childish things so
gravely now,
When war or peace hangs on them? There
are Catholics
In England still. They still plot against our
queen.
Were she struck down by one of them
you'd take
Her throne and rule us. It follows that your
faith
Is a challenge to her—yes, if your Grace
will pardon
The word—a defiance.

MARY

You were bid to say this to me?

THROGMORTON

Madame, it was said so smoothly by my
queen
There was no offense in it, but I have no
gift
Of language. I must say things out.

MARY

Your manner
Is packed with the most magniloquent im-
pudence
That's come my way. Do you or your
queenly mistress
Deem me an inferior, to be given orders
blithely,
With a high hand?

THROGMORTON

No, madame.

MARY

Say three words more
In this cavalier offensive style of yours
And you'll find yourself in the courtyard.

THROGMORTON

Madame, I—

MARY

Come down to earth, and speak without
swaggering.

THROGMORTON

I've been in the wrong.

MARY

That's better.

THROGMORTON

It's true that I'd
Rehearsed my song and dance. Your wit is
quicker
Than's been supposed in London.

MARY

Quick enough.
To perceive an insult, I hope.

THROGMORTON

Your Majesty,
There was none intended, but I might have
spoken more wisely
Had I known your mettle. Elizabeth is
concerned,
As I have said, with the differences that are
certain
To arise over your religion. Further than
that,
What arrangements may be made to avert
a breach

In the present concord, if we may discuss
these things
Frankly, and you will make frank replies, I
have
No other mission.

MARY

Now you talk sense. And frankly.
I will not change my faith.

THROGMORTON

And, frankly again,
There was little hope that you would.
There is some hope,
However, that when Your Majesty seeks a
consort
You will not do so to bolster up your claim
To the English crown, which is strong
enough already
To cause us uneasiness in London.

MARY

That
Had not occurred to me.

THROGMORTON

But surely your choice in marriage
Will imply your attitude?

MARY

I have no intention
Of plighting my troth at once, but if I had
I've received advice already on that point,
A mort of it—and I'm tender.

THROGMORTON

Say no more,
Madame, and I'll say no more.

MARY

Oh, out with it now,
Give the advice. I won't take it.

THROGMORTON

Why, it's only this:
If Your Majesty were to marry a Protestant
lord
Of no royal pretensions, it would indicate
That you meant no danger to our Eliza-
beth.

MARY

She has chosen for me, I daresay? She has
some lord
Of the sort in mind?

- - -

THROGMORTON

You embarrass me to go on.
She mentioned a name.

MARY

Yes?

THROGMORTON

Madame, the Earl of Leicester.

MARY

I hope her ears burn now. Leicester? Her
cast-off!—
Her favorite—the one she's dangled? This
is an affront—
She named Lord Leicester?

THROGMORTON

Nay, nay—only to show you
What it was she had in mind. The kind of
match.

MARY

I would hope so.

THROGMORTON

For, you see, Your Majesty,
She had a fear of this—the young Lord
Darnley
Has come north against her will. Why he's
here we don't know.
Nor whether by invitation, nor what your
plans
Might be concerning him.

MARY

I have none.

THROGMORTON

Then, if you will,
Forget what I've said. It was only that this
Darnley
Combines to exactness what Elizabeth
dreads
In case you marry. After you he's next to
her throne,
And he's a Catholic. Should you marry
Lord Darnley
And call up Catholic Europe to your
back—
Well, we'd be ringed in steel.

MARY

I have offered your queen
My friendship and love. I meant that offer.

THROGMORTON

But even
If there were no quarrel, and you should
marry Darnley
And have a son by him—he'd be heir to
England—
And I think the plain fact is that Elizabeth
Would rather choose her own heir.

MARY

Now God forgive me!—
I am heir to the throne of England, and
after me
Whatever children I have—unless by some
chance
The virgin queen should bear sons! Is it
part of her love
To cut me off from my right?

THROGMORTON

It must be remembered
That England is Protestant, and it might
come hard
To accept a Romish sovereign. In brief, my
queen
Has wished that you might choose Both-
well, or perhaps some other
Of Protestant persuasion!

MARY

And that's the message.
We're down to it at last. My lord Throg-
morton,
I marry where I please—whether now or
later,
And I abate not one jot of my good blood's
lien
On the English throne. Nay, knowing now
the gist
Of Elizabeth's polity toward that claim, I
shall rather
Strengthen it if I can. The least worthy
sovereign
Has a duty toward his blood, not to weak-
en it
Nor let it decline in place.

THROGMORTON

This will hardly please.

MARY

I could hardly expect it would. But I too
am a power,

And it matters what pleases me. This was
    all?

THROGMORTON

This was all
I'm commissioned with.

MARY

I shall see to your safe-conduct.

THROGMORTON

I thank your Majesty.
(*He goes out.* MARY *is alone a moment,
brooding.* RIZZIO *enters.*)

MARY

Oh, Rizzio, Rizzio,
They make a mock of me! It was as you
    predicted
To the utter syllable.

RIZZIO

A warning, then.

MARY

We'll expect no friendship from England.
She cuts me off, me and my line.

RIZZIO

May I say that this
Is only her wish, not accomplished?

MARY

Aye, and not to be.
I'd have stood her friend, Rizzio, meant to
    be her friend,
But now—this is not to be borne! Go and
    find Lord Darnley.

RIZZIO

Your Majesty—you have made a decision?

MARY

Yes.

RIZZIO

Now I thank you. Now, God helping us,
    we'll win.
She'll not stamp you out.

MARY

So I think. And now find him.

RIZZIO

Yes.
(MARY BEATON *comes to the outer door.*)

BEATON

Will your Majesty see a gentleman calling
    himself Lord Bothwell?
(BOTHWELL *comes to the door.*)

MARY

He's in again?

BEATON

There's no keeping him out.

BOTHWELL

(*Entering*). The doxy invited me in her-
    self. She's a slut,
This Beaton of yours.
(RIZZIO *goes out the outer door.*)

MARY

Oh, I know.

BEATON

May I put in a word
For this gentleman, madame? Of all who
    come calling on you
He's the most ill-favored. It may be that
    he's honest,
I hope so, to go with that face. You're not
    afraid
To be left alone with him?

MARY

You may go, Beaton.

BEATON

Yes, Majesty.
(*She curtsies hurriedly, and goes out.*)

BOTHWELL

Now, what an inexperienced queen you are
To surround yourself with such taking
    bitches!

MARY

My lord,
I have heard from England.

BOTHWELL

Mary, my queen, what you heard

I could have guessed. She's your demon.
She bodes you ill.

MARY

I believe it now.

BOTHWELL

And moreover, between the two,
This cormorant brother of yours, and that
English harpy
They'll have the heart out of you, and
share it. Trust
Not one word they say to you, trust not
. even the anger
Their words rouse in you. They calculate
effects.

MARY

Where is Lord Morton?

BOTHWELL

Lord Morton is not well.
(*He is very serious.*)
A sudden indisposition.

MARY

Bothwell, Bothwell—
You've fought with him!

BOTHWELL

A mere puncture. What men think
I cannot punish, nor what they say elsewhere but when
I hear them, by Christ, they'll learn manners.

MARY

I forbade it.

BOTHWELL

Forbade it! My dear, not God nor the holy
angels
Forbid me when I'm angry.

MARY

I say I forbade it
It's I who's responsible for my kingdom—
not you—
You were bound to keep the peace!

BOTHWELL

When my lady's slandered?
I'll teach them to hold their peace where
you're concerned
Or find their sweet peace in heaven.

MARY

Would God I'd been born
Deep somewhere in the Highlands, and
there met you—
A maid in your path, and you but a High-
land bowman
Who needed me.

BOTHWELL

Why, if you love me, Marie,
You're my maid and I your soldier.

MARY

And it won't be.

BOTHWELL

Aye, it will be.

MARY

For, hear me, my lord of Bothwell.
I too have a will—a will as strong as your
own.
And enemies of my own, and my long re-
venges
To carry through. I will have my way in
my time
Though it burn my heart out and yours.
The gods set us tasks,
My lord, what we must do.

BOTHWELL

Let me understand you.
The gods, supposing there are such, have
thrown us together
Somewhat, of late.

MARY

Look, Bothwell. I am a sovereign,
And you obey no one. Were I married to
you I'd be
Your woman to sleep with. You'd be king
here in Edinburgh,
And I'd have no mind to your ruling.

BOTHWELL

They'll beat you alone.
Together we could cope them.

MARY

Love you I may—
Love you I have—but not now, and no
more. It's for me
To rule, not you. I'll deliver up no land
To such a hot-head. If you'd been born to
the blood

I'd say, aye, take it, the heavens had a
   meaning in this,
But the royal blood's in me.—It's to me
   they turn
To keep the peace, patch up old quarrels,
   bring home
Old exiles, make a truce to anarchy. Escape
   it I cannot.
Delegate it I cannot. The blame's my own
For whatever's done in my name.—I will
   have no master.
(BOTHWELL *is silent when she pauses.*)
Nay, I am jealous of this my Stuart blood.
Jealous of what it has meant in Scotland,
   jealous
Of what it may mean. They've attacked
   that blood, and I'm angry.
They'll meet more anger than they know.

BOTHWELL

And who
Has angered you? Not I?

MARY

Elizabeth.

BOTHWELL

I thought so.
She's afraid, if I'm half a prophet,
That you'll marry me.

MARY

Her fears run the other way.
She's afraid I'll marry a Catholic and
   threaten her throne!
She threatens disinheritance! Offers me
   Leicester!
Her leavings!

BOTHWELL

Yes, by God, that's a cold potato.

MARY

And means to choose another heir for her
   throne!
I may never sit on it, but the Stuart line
Shall not suffer by me!

BOTHWELL

Will you tell me what that means?

MARY

I mean if I have a son he'll govern England.

BOTHWELL

And so he might, if he were mine, too.

MARY

Nay, might—
But it must be!
She dares to threaten my heritage!

BOTHWELL

Does that mean Lord Darnley?
(*She is silent.*)
Aye, lady, will you stoop so low to choose
A weapon? This is not worthy of the girl
I've known. Am I to be ousted by a popinjay
Who drinks in the morning and cannot
   carry his drink?
An end of mouldy string? You take too
   much
On yourself of the future. Think of us,
   and the hours
Close on us here we might have together.
   Leave something
To the gods in heaven! They look after
   lovers!

MARY

Oh, what's a little love, a trick of the eyes,
A liking, to be set beside the name
You'll have forever, or your son will have?

BOTHWELL

Well, it's been nibbling at you this long
   while,
And now it's got you, the blight of Charle-
   magne—
The itch to conquer.

MARY

I have an itch to conquer?

BOTHWELL

It goes deep, too, that itch. It eats out the
   brain.

MARY

Well, and my love for you, how worthy is
   that?
It's my body wants you. Something I've
   fought against
Comes out in me when you're near. You've
   not held it sacred.
You've taken others. I've known. And then
   come wooing.
It would happen again.

BOTHWELL

It's a man's way. I've loved you
None the less.

MARY

You don't offer enough, Lord Bothwell.
You're not true in it, and I'm not true to
myself
In what I feel for you.

BOTHWELL

I'm no lute-player,
To languish and write sonnets when my
lady
Says me nay. Faith, I've lived rough on the
border,
And cut some throats. I don't forgive my-
self
Too easily, when I look back, but I tell you
If I give my pledge to you it's an honest
pledge,
And I'll keep it. Yes, and when the tug
begins
Around your throne, you'll be lost without
me. Try
No threats toward England.—It will tax a
hardy man
All his time to hold what you have.

MARY

We differ there, too.
What I have I'll defend for myself.

BOTHWELL

If you marry this Darnley
I take away my hand.

MARY

Before God, he believes
He's held me up so far, and I'd fall without
him!

BOTHWELL

I believe it, and it's true! Darnley, sweet
Christ!
No miracle could make him a king! He's a
punk,
And he'll rule like a punk!

MARY

We shall see, Lord Bothwell.

BOTHWELL

Well, I'm sped. My suit's cold. But, dod,
lady—Darnley—

He sticks in my craw—I can't go him.
You'll find few that can.
Think twice about that. Let him not cross
my way,
Or he'll lose his plumes like Morton!

MARY

Will you learn, Lord Bothwell,
That this is not your palace, but mine? Or
must you
Be taught that lesson?

BOTHWELL

There's been a bond between us
We'll find it hard to forget.

MARY

You may. Not I.
I've set my face where I'm going.
(RIZZIO *enters.* DARNLEY *is seen behind
him.*)

RIZZIO

Lord Darnley is here,
Your Majesty.

MARY

Let him enter.
(DARNLEY *enters from the doorway.*)

BOTHWELL

Lass, lass, God fend thee.
You've seen the last of me.

MARY

I've given no leave
For departure, Lord Bothwell!

BOTHWELL

I need no leave, nor leave-taking.
You see no more of me.
(*He goes out.* RIZZIO *bows and follows him.*
MARY *crosses the room away from* DARNLEY
*and looks for a moment in the fire. Then
she turns to him.*)

MARY

I have sent for you.
Lord Darnley, to tell you your suit has
prospered. You've asked
My hand in marriage, and I grant it.

DARNLEY

Your Majesty—
I hardly hoped—I haven't dared—this is
fortune
To take one's breath!

(*He comes forward and falls to one knee.*)
I shall love you, keep you, defend you!

MARY

We shall face troubled times.

DARNLEY

We'll meet them bravely.
This is some dream—or a jest. It can't be.

MARY

Aye. I feel that.
And yet it's true.

DARNLEY

I'm to hold you in my arms!

MARY

Not yet. And yet, if you like, come, kiss
me.

DARNLEY

They say
A kiss seals the bargain!
(*He rises, staggering slightly.*)

MARY

I've heard so.
(*He crosses to her.*)
You've drunk too much.

DARNLEY

Nay, only a morning cup. Oh, Lady, lady—
When you're kind the whole world's kind!

MARY

(*She faces him, then draws back a step in
repulsion.*)
You're a boy, a child.

DARNLEY

Older than you, though.
It's a bargain, then?

MARY

Yes.
(*He puts out his arms to her. Her eyes hold
him off.*)
Let the kissing go. Let it go till the bond's
sealed.

DARNLEY

Aye, madame.
(*He drops his arms. They stand looking at
each other.*)
                              Curtain

ACT TWO

SCENE I

SCENE: *The hall in the palace. Evening.* MARY *and the* FOUR MARY'S-IN-WAITING *are sitting
near the fire, listening as* RIZZIO *sings to his lute.*

RIZZIO

My heart's in the north,
And my life's in the south,
False I've pledged with my hand,
False I've kissed with my mouth.

Oh, would we might lie
Where we lay by the firth,
With one cloak about us,
To keep us from earth,

With hand caught to hand
And the rain driving blind,

As the new years have driven
Old love out of mind.

MARY

What is the line, False I've pledged with
my hand?

RIZZIO

False I've pledged with my hand,
False I've kissed with my mouth.

MARY

Where did you come by the song?

MARY

Look, what can one say to him? You ask him a question—and he threatens you with the Last Judgment! You see, Master Knox, you are not the judge who will sit over us in the Last Judgment! You are instead an elderly gentleman of provincial learning and fanatical beliefs, lately married to a niece of your own some forty years your junior, and one who conducts his conversations almost exclusively in quotations from the Old Testament. If you will talk sensibly with me I shall talk sensibly with you, but if you come here to frighten me I shall regard you as a most ridiculous antediluvian figure, and find you very funny. Which shall it be?

KNOX

Well I know you hold the Lord God as a jest and a mockery!

MARY

Do not confuse yourself with Lord God again! There's a difference!

KNOX

I am His spokesman.
(RIZZIO *comes to the door.*)

MARY

Indeed. Will you show me your commission?

KNOX

I call ruin to fall on this house, the shelter of the great beast—!

MARY

And there again! Maitland, can you, by any stretch of the imagination, look upon me as the great beast?

RIZZIO

Your Majesty, Lord Huntley is here.

MARY

Come in, Lord Huntley!
(HUNTLEY *enters.*)
Sir, I have just heard myself likened to the great beast of Revelations. Can you see any similarity there?

HUNTLEY

Why, lass, I'd say at the least it's an exaggeration.

MAITLAND

If Your Majesty wishes to give audience to Lord Huntley—
(*He starts to withdraw.*)

MARY

Nay, why should you go? And why should John Knox and Lord Huntley not meet face to face in one room? I am aware that Master Knox is a Protestant and that Huntley is a Catholic, but they dwell in the same kingdom, and it would be well if they understood each other.

KNOX

I am loath to say it, but I am of a mind that there can be no understanding between him and me, no, nor between myself and Your Majesty, lest I betray my Lord.

HUNTLEY

Madame, it's my opinion we understand each other dom well. Too dom well.

MARY

But since you must both live in this kingdom and one must be Catholic and one Protestant, surely it were wiser to be amiable over small matters, Maitland?

MAITLAND

Aye, it would be wiser.

KNOX

Not for what you have said to me or of my person, for that unto seventy times seven those who follow him forgive, but because the air of this house is offensive in his nostrils, I call ruin on it! Nor will I commune in it further, neither with those who make their beds here nor with those who come here for counsel! Yea, if there are any here who would avoid the wrath, let them turn now, for it is upon you and your servants!

MARY

Well—it would seem there's little to be done about that. You are dismissed if you wish to go.
(MAITLAND *and* KNOX *turn to leave.*)

MAITLAND

I offer my apologies, Your Majesty.

MARY

Oh, surely.

KNOX

Yea, those who breed and take their ease
in the places of the anointed, turn, turn
now, before the axe fall quickly and be followed by silence! For now it is not too late,
but no man knows when he cometh, nor
on the wings of what morning!
(MAITLAND and KNOX *go out.* RIZZIO *rejoins
the group at the fire.*)

MARY

You are duly impressed by this talk, sir?

BEATON

Why, the solemn ass! He should have been
booted!

HUNTLEY

My dear, you've been too easy with him,
and if you continue to be easy we'll pay for
it.

MARY

And in what way, sir?

HUNTLEY

You and I are alone here, Your Majesty, so
far as Catholicism's concerned. My High-
landers are Catholic, it's true, and there's
a plenty of them, and they're tough, but
the rest are all against us, every noble and
man of note. They're John Knox's men,
and you heard yourself what he said.

BEATON

He with the persimmon-colored whiskers?

HUNTLEY

Aye, he. And he means it.

MARY

What does he mean?

HUNTLEY

Ruin to this house.

MARY

Is this a house to be blown down with
windy talk?

HUNTLEY

My birdie—I canna call you Ye're Majesty
and all that—

MARY

You need not.

HUNTLEY

Then, my bird, they draw their nets tight
about us. I told you before, and it's coming.

MARY

And who draws the net?

HUNTLEY

(*Looking at the others*). Lady—

MARY

These five know my secret heart. They'll
say nothing.

HUNTLEY

Lady, there's only one defence. Attack
them first. And there's but one proper place
for John Knox. He should be in Edinburgh
Castle—and all those with him who are of
his mind.

MARY

You'd imprison him?

HUNTLEY

He and some twenty others.

MARY

And then?

HUNTLEY

Then you can go to work. You're not safe
here and I'm not safe here while a sect of
Protestant lords divide your dominion with
you. You rule by sufferance only.

MARY

They are here by my sufferance, Huntley.

HUNTLEY

You have heard of the sheep nursed the
wolf-pups till they tore her to pieces.

MARY

But we're not sheep and wolves, my lord.
There's room for all of us here, and for
whatever faiths we may choose to have.

HUNTLEY

Never think it, my bird, never believe it!
It's never yet happened that a state sur-

vived with two religions in it. Never. Elizabeth knows that. She's behind this Knox. He'd never dare be so bold if she weren't behind him.

MARY

But it's my thought that in Scotland, though it be the first time in the world, we shall all believe as we please and worship as we list. And Elizabeth may take it as she sees fit.

HUNTLEY

She uses it against you, my dear, and uses John Knox against you. Ladybird, I'm willing to beg it of you, take heed of me now or we're both done!

MARY

Rizzio?

RIZZIO

You know my mind. I'm with Lord Huntley in this.

MARY

But how can I bring myself to imprison men for no wrong they've done, on suspicion only, imprison them for their faith?

HUNTLEY

It's more than faith. It's works. You heard John Knox!

MARY

It cuts athwart every right instinct I have, my lord! Every fibre I have that's royal shrinks at such pennywise petty doings! And John Knox—a doddering imbecile, drooling prophecy!

HUNTLEY

He threatened you, lady.

MARY

No, no, I can't. Even if it were wisdom to do it, and it's not.
(*The right-hand door opens suddenly and* DARNLEY *stands in it.* MARY *turns toward him.*)
My lord!
(DARNLEY *walks slowly to the middle of the room and lays a hand on the table.*)

DARNLEY

I'm unexpected, perhaps? Too early? A thought
Too early? I'll retire. Come when I'm wanted.

MARY

No,
My lord, you've been long expected, and more than welcome.

DARNLEY

Why, a pretty wife, a huswife with her maids;
A pretty sight, and maybe a cavalier
Or two, for the maids' company. Dod, sit down, all!
Damn me if I'll intrude!

MARY

Will you speak to Lord Huntley?

DARNLEY

(*Focusing on* HUNTLEY).
Right. That's right. Lord Huntley, give me your hand.
I thank you for watching over the pretty wife here.
I've been away.

HUNTLEY

(*Turning*). Your Majesty, you've a wife
Such as I wish I'd had when I was young.

DARNLEY

Right—You have right. They all say that.
I'd say it myself,
Only I know her better.
(*He turns to the door.*)
I know her too well.
And not well enough. She wouldn't care to hear it.
Not from me.

MARY

Darnley.

DARNLEY

She sleeps alone.
At least as far as I know.

HUNTLEY

I'll take my leave,
My lady.

MARY

Yes.

DARNLEY

Stay, stay, I'm going. I only
Tell you she sleeps alone as far as I know.
A pretty wife. These women—they get
with child,
You never know how—and then they
won't sleep with you.
(HUNTLEY *bows to* MARY, *turns deliberate-
ly, and goes out the door to the right, clos-
ing it.*)
What's the matter with him? He's an old
married man.
He knows these things.

MARY

You're tired, my lord. Will you wish
Some service, something to eat and drink?

DARNLEY

She sends me
Off to bed, you note. You note it, Rizzio?
There's a service she could do me, but I
doubt
She'll offer it. And I'm a king, by God, a
king,
And you're a clark by office!

MARY

My lord, I hoped
You'd have some other word for me when
you
Returned.

DARNLEY

My pink, if I gave you the word you've
earned
The room would smell. I've been at the
hunting. We had
Something to drink. Alban! Alban! Allons!

MARY

You call some one?

DARNLEY

Alban! God's right! St. Andrew! Alban!
I'm drunk, you see.

MARY

I think not.

DARNLEY

Yes, but I am.
Alban! Christ his sonties, am I left
Alone here! God and St. Andrew!

(*The right-hand door opens and* RUTHVEN
enters in full armor.)

MARY

What is this?
(*To* RUTHVEN.)
You will retire, sir. Who are you?

DARNLEY

My good friend Ruthven.

MARY

Is this a place for armor? I will receive
Lord Ruthven another time.

DARNLEY

The callant's there,
Ruthven.

RUTHVEN

Aye.

MARY

I had heard that Lord Ruthven was ill,
And thought to go to him, not to see him
here.

RUTHVEN

I am ill, and it's mortal, but I've sworn to
be mortal
To another first.

MARY

This is my apartment, sir,
And I ask you to go.
(DOUGLAS *appears behind* RUTHVEN.)

MARY

I demand little courtesy,
But that little I must have. Are these your
friends?
If so, take them elsewhere.

DARNLEY

Aye, I'm to have my friends
In my apartment—and you're to have
yours here.
I say no—they're to mingle.—
(*He points to* RIZZIO.)
You see that grig
With the kinked hair there? He with the
lady's hands
And feet? Where does he sleep nights?
That's he, that's the one
We have in question!

MARY

My lord, when you've been drinking
I have little taste for your company, and to-
night
Less, perhaps, than ever.

DARNLEY

He, he, I tell you!
That Italian spawn!
(RIZZIO, *trembling, steps back toward the
queen's study.*)

MARY

(*Stepping in front of* RIZZIO).
Go into my study.
(LORD MORTON *enters.*)
Lord Morton,
Whatever you have in hand here, put no
faith
In this king I've crowned and set beside
me! His word
Is a paper shield.

DARNLEY

I'm king in this country, mistress—
And I know my rights.

MARY

Beaton, why were these men
Not stopped at my door?

DARNLEY

They came with me.

BEATON

(*Facing* MORTON).
Will you tell me
What you want with the queen?

MORTON

(*His dagger drawn*). Damme, do you
want this bodkin
Through that bodice of yours?
(*She shrinks back.* RIZZIO, *having reached
the study step by step, opens it and reveals
a* GUARD, *a drawn claymore in his hand.*)

RIZZIO

Let me pass!

THE GUARD

Nay, lad.

FLEMING

Your Majesty,
They've broken into your rooms.
(MARY *turns and sees the guard.*)

MARY

Lord Darnley, was that
By your order?

RIZZIO

(*Hardly able to speak for fear*). Save me,
my queen, save me!

MARY

Aye, Rizzio.
(*The five women retreat before the armed
men, covering* RIZZIO *from them.*)

MORTON

Look to the women-folk, Darnley. We'll
care for him.
(RIZZIO *turns suddenly and leaps behind
the heavy drapes of the high window
down-stage.* MORTON, DOUGLAS *and* RUTH-
VEN *follow him,* DOUGLAS *with his dagger
raised.*)

MARY

Douglas, I'll remember this!
(*A fall is heard behind the curtains, but no
cry.* MARY *runs toward the window, but is
met by* RUTHVEN, *sheathing his dagger.*)
You've murdered him!
You pack of filthy cowards!

RUTHVEN

Yea, and done well.

MARY

Done well! Oh, fools and cowards!
(*She runs to the curtain and with* MARY
BEATON *pulls it back from* RIZZIO, *then
bends over him and draws back again in
terror.*)
Oh, David, David,
It was I wouldn't let you go!

DARNLEY

(*Looking away*). You might cover that
sight.

MARY

Is he dead, Beaton?

BEATON

Yes, madame.

MARY

Oh, you do well, you do well,
All of you!

(*She conquers her repulsion, and tries to loosen* RIZZIO'S *ruff.* FLEMING *comes to help her.*)
We'll help him if we can,
Fleming.

FLEMING

Yes.

MARY

You were too gentle for them,
David. They couldn't bear it—these boors and swine—
Your kerchief, Fleming! He bleeds so—

FLEMING

It's useless, madame.

MARY

(*Rising*). Yes.
(*To the lords.*) To take him unarmed, and poniard him—
One who had never hurt you!

RUTHVEN

(*Sinking to a chair*). Well, the work's done,
And my queen's wiped clear of him.

MARY

Wiped clear! You believed
I was guilty with him!

RUTHVEN

Were you not?

MARY

No!

RUTHVEN

I'd be sorry
If you were not. I struck him down for that.

MARY

I was not guilty. But will you tell me now
Who'll believe me innocent? You've branded me deep
With this murder, and you've killed a guiltless man!
Why do you sit in my presence?

RUTHVEN

Because I'm ill
And dying. I should be sorry if this thing
I've done were in error—for it's the last I'll do.

MARY

You'll stand in my presence! Whose order was it?

RUTHVEN

Why, ask His Majesty that—
And Morton there, and Moray.
(*He rises with difficulty.*)

MARY

Moray too?

RUTHVEN

Yea, your brother. For me—let me go home.

MARY

Go. Morton and Douglas, I give you three days
To leave this kingdom.

MORTON

And the king? I have the king's seal
For what I've done.

MARY

Is that true?

DARNLEY

Aye.

MARY

The worse for you.
The worse for you all.

DARNLEY

My lady, this long while past
You've denied me your chamber, and when I've seen you there's been
This Rizzio with you.

MARY

Never again while I live
Will you see me alone. I bear your child in me
Or you'd answer for this!

DARNLEY

There'll be no answering!
We know what we know about you!

MARY

I would I knew
In what strange dark chamber of your oafish brain

You found reasons for Rizzio's death. If I
saw you seldom
Remember how often you drank yourself
imbecile
Before you came to me. You've slain your
last friend, sir.
It was Rizzio's counsel put you where you
are
And kept you there. These are not your
friends, these three,
Nor Moray. They wanted Rizzio out of
the way,
And they wanted to drag you down, and
drag me down,
And you play into their hands. I've never
been
Unfaithful to you, but we're at an end, we
two.
From this time forward if I touch your
hand
May God blight me and my child!

DARNLEY

I wanted you!
You kept away from me, and it drove me
mad!

MARY

You won't mend it now. Look, young Riz-
zio's dead,
You've blackened me, blackened yourself,
thrown a black doubt
On the child who'll be your heir. The lords
look on
And smile, knowing they've trapped you.
You'll never climb
From the pit where you've fallen, and I
may fall with you. Lord Moray
Weaves his web round us. You've helped
him.

DARNLEY

God knows I wanted
Only my right.

MARY

You pitiful dolt! To think
Such a calf should rule, and at my choos-
ing! God
May forgive you—not I. Nor forgive my-
self.—And Rizzio.—
Take yourselves out! You pollute the dead
to stand there!
He wanted to go to Italy.

FLEMING

Yes.

MARY

Will you go?
(MORTON *beckons the guards, and they
cross from the study to the outer door.*)

RUTHVEN

(*At the door*). You'll want some help,
mayhap.

MARY

None of yours. I've noticed
It's men that kill, but women that wash
the corpse
And weep for it. May none ever weep for
you.

RUTHVEN

None will. I've been in the wrong.

MARY

I'm sorry, Lord Ruthven.
It's an ill thing to have on your heart when
you die.

RUTHVEN

Aye, is it.
(*He goes out, and the men follow him.*
DARNLEY *looks back as if he wished to
speak to the queen, but goes silently.*)

MARY

And now we're alone. The lords have
shown their hand.
Rizzio's gone—and Darnley, what there
was to go.
We've been not long in Scotland, but time
enough
To show I can lose it, have lost it in their
minds
Already. We must lay the poor lad somewhere.
Could we lift him together?

SETON

Oh, madame, I'm afraid!

MARY

Of what?

SETON

I've never seen one dead before.
I've not known it was like this.

MARY

It's poor Rizzio.
No one to hurt us. And you and I will lie
Some time like this, and folk will be afraid
Because we lie so still. How strange it is
That he should frighten us who wished us
well,
And would still if he lived. We must take
him up
And lay him on my bed. I'll sleep with
Beaton
Tonight.
(*She takes a step toward* RIZZIO.)

BEATON

Madame, the blood will stain your dress.

MARY

If that were all. This will bring more blood
after.
Now I see it. Before I reign here clearly
There will be many men lie so for me   .
Slain in needless quarrel. Slain, and each
one
With blood to spill but once, like his. And
yet
One steps on into it—steps from life to life
Till there are thousands dead, and goes on
still
Till the heart faints and sickens, and still
goes on
And must go on.
(*An iron gate clangs outside.* BEATON *parts
the curtains to look out.*)
I tell you, Fleming, my soul
Is aghast at this blood spilled for me, and
yet
It hardens me, too. These are their man-
ners, this
Is the way they go to work. I shall work on
them,
And not too lightly. They think of me as a
girl,
Afraid of them. They shall see.—And yet
my mind
Believes nothing of what I say; I'm weak
as grief,
Stripped and wept out before them. They
press me close,
And I have no one to send.
(*There is a rattle of staves in the court-
yard.*)

BEATON

(*Turning back*). It's the provost, madame,
I heard them call his name.

MARY

He's not to enter.
Let no one enter.
(BEATON *goes out right.*)
No one. In all this kingdom.
I can trust only five, and one's myself,
And we're women, all of us.—If they go
scot-free
After this indignity I'm no queen. For
Ruthven,
He'll pay his own score. He's dying. Mor-
ton and Douglas
Must die too.

FLEMING

They were under Lord Darnley's orders.

MARY

He was under theirs. It won't save them

FLEMING

Your Majesty,
They've left the city by now. They should
have been taken
While they were in your hands.

MARY

I know. It's true.
They've fled to raise troops. When next we
find them they'll meet us
With culverins.
(BEATON *enters.*)
He's gone?

BEATON

Yes. But there's one
Below from France—says he has news.

MARY

From France?
Tomorrow, though. I wish I were still in
France
And had never seen these stone walls.

LIVINGSTONE

And so do I.

MARY

What is his name?

BEATON

He gave me
This token for you, no name. It's a crow's
feather.

MARY

(*Takes the feather, then pauses*). Tell my
  Lord Bothwell I have no wish to see him.
Now or later.

BEATON

Madame, you'll see him? I brought him
Along with me.

MARY

No. Not now. Not ever.
There's nothing to say between us now.

BEATON

He came
From France to see you.

MARY

Tell him.
(LORD BOTHWELL *is seen standing in the*
doorway.)

BOTHWELL

Your Majesty,
You've had unwelcome company this hour,
If I've heard aright, and I care not to be
  another,
But I come to make an offer I made be-
  fore—
To be your soldier.

MARY

I have no time to talk,
Lord Bothwell. Nor do I wish to see you.
  The time's
Gone by.

BOTHWELL

My queen, my queen, turn not away
Your friends. You've few enough, too few
  it seems
To prevent what's happened.

MARY

Go.

BOTHWELL

Does he still lie here?
I'll lay the poor boy away for you at least,
And then I'll go, since you wish it.
(*He crosses to* RIZZIO.)
Aye, they made sure,
Lad—and their dirks were sharp. Shall I
  place him within?

MARY

Yes.
(BOTHWELL *picks up* RIZZIO *and carries him*
into MARY's *chamber*.)
Must you betray me, too?

BEATON

I wished only—
If you'd but follow your heart!

MARY

We two must twain,
My Beaton. You take too much on you.
  Lord Bothwell,
May be your friend, not mine.

BEATON

Forgive me.

MARY

What warrant
Have you been given to vouch for my
  heart, or judge
Whether I should follow it?

BEATON

None.

MARY

Oh, God, this vice
Of women, crying and tears! To weep,
  weep now
When I need my anger! Say my farewells
  for me,
I've gone to my study.
(*She turns.* BOTHWELL *enters*.)

BOTHWELL

Good night, my queen.

MARY

Good night.
I'm not unkind. But I'm cut off from you.
You know that.

BOTHWELL

Yes. There's no need to hide your weeping.
He was over-young to die.

MARY

It's not for him.
No, it's for all I wanted my life to be,
And is not.

BOTHWELL

Majesty, you have a fortunate star.
It will come well yet.

MARY

If I have a star at all
It's an evil one. To violate my room,
Kill my servants before my eyes—How I
    must be hated!

BOTHWELL

They'll pay for that.

MARY

Perhaps.

BOTHWELL

I've taken an oath
They'll pay for it. Your Majesty, I wearied
Of France and exile, wearied of sun and
    wine,
And looked north over the water, longing
    for fog
And heather and my own country. Further,
    the news
Was none too happy from Scotland. They
    want your throne
And plan to have it. But I mean to live in
    this land
And mean you to be queen of it. The Earl
    of Bothwell
Is home, and spoiling for a fight. Before
Day dawns they'll hear from me.

MARY

My lord, I thank you—

BOTHWELL

Give me no thanks. I like a fight too well
To pretend it's a virtue. Moreover, if I'm to
    live here
I'd rather you were my liege than Moray.
    I'm none
So fond of your half-brother. This night's
    work
Should show you he's what I knew him,
    half-bred, half-faced
And double-tongued.

MARY

You have no army.

BOTHWELL

I have
My border men. Lord Huntley's joined
    with me

With his Highland kilties. If you'd call
    your clans
We could drive them to the wall.

MARY

It's a war then.

BOTHWELL

It's war,
Already. They've turned your Darnley
    against you. They'll use him
As long as they need his seal. Once they've
    got you out
They'll set Moray up as regent. They fear
    one chance:
That you and I should league together and
    balk them.
I've come back in time, not too soon.

MARY

I think you have.
My lord, I had no heart to face you. The
    fault
Was mine when we parted.

BOTHWELL

It's not too late. I've come
Only just in time, but in time.

MARY

It is too late—
For you and me. These faults we commit
    have lives
Of their own, and bind us to them.

BOTHWELL

(Pointing toward her bedroom). Yon was
    Darnley's work.
Are you still his?

MARY

Am I not?
(BEATON gathers up the three others with a
look and goes into the queen's study with
them silently.)
I'm to bear his child.
I cannot hate my child.

BOTHWELL

It's in the wind
This Darnley's not to live long.

MARY

I'd have no hand
In that—nor you!

BOTHWELL

It happens he's a pawn
In the game the lords are playing. They'll
  sacrifice him
When the time comes. It's no plot of mine.

MARY

But he lives
And I'm his wife, and my babe is his. I
  must drink
My cup down to the rinse. It was I that
  filled it,
And if there's grief at the bottom it's mine.
  I'll name you
My officer, but only if you can pledge
No harm will come through you to Darn-
  ley.

BOTHWELL

Lady,
I need you, and you need me, but I'll be
  damned
If Darnley's needed on this earth. I have
No project against him, but I'll give no
  pledge
To block me if I should have. There be
  men
Who wear their welcome out in this world
  early,
And Darnley's one of them.

MARY

You have never yet
Learned how to take an order.

BOTHWELL

And never will—
From man or woman living, sovereign or
  knave,
Judge or vicegerent. I have not been con-
  quered
And will not be. But I offer you my fealty,
And it's worth the more for that.

MARY

You must make your own terms—
I'm but a beggar here.

BOTHWELL

Nay, nay, it's I
That sue, a beggar for what's impossible,
With this Darnley standing between us.
(*She pauses again.*)

MARY

You shall be
My Lord Admiral, and act for me. Yes, and
  to that
Let me add how my breath caught when I
  knew you here,
Hoping I know not what, things not to be,
Hopes I must strangle down. Oh, Both-
  well, Bothwell!
I was wrong! I loved you all the time, and
  denied you!
Forgive me—even too late!

BOTHWELL

I tell you we
Shall be happy yet.

MARY

No, for I think I've been
At the top of what I'll have, and all the rest
Is going down. It's as if a queen should
  stand
High up, at the head of a stair—I see this
  now
As in a dream—and she in her dream
  should step
From level to level downward, all this
  while knowing
She should mount and not descend—till at
  last she walks
An outcast in the courtyard—bayed at by
  dogs
That were her hunters—walks there in
  harsh morning
And the dream's done.

BOTHWELL

(*Stepping toward her*). You're weary.
  You've borne too much.
They shall pay for this.

MARY

Come no nearer, my lord. It's not ours
To have. Go now.

BOTHWELL

Yes, your Majesty.
(*He turns.*) Yet
I tell you we shall be happy. And there will
  be nothing
Not ours to have.
(*He goes out.*)

Curtain

SCENE II

SCENE: ELIZABETH'S *study at Whitehall.* BURGHLEY *and* ELIZABETH *are seated across a table.*
A THIRD FIGURE *approaches from the side.*

BURGHLEY

This will be Lord Throgmorton.

ELIZABETH

You're early, sir.

THROGMORTON

Madame, I rode all night.—I've news from
the north.
Darnley's been murdered.

ELIZABETH

How?

THROGMORTON

Kirk o' Field was blown up.
The castle's in ruins.

ELIZABETH

Now that was a waste of powder—
And of castles too. But he's dead—

THROGMORTON

Yes, madame—they found him.
It was no accident. He'd been strangled.

ELIZABETH

So there's no more king in Scotland.
Who took this trouble?

THROGMORTON

Moray, and Morton, no doubt—perhaps
Maitland—

ELIZABETH

Not Bothwell?—

THROGMORTON

No—though he must have known of it—

ELIZABETH

And the queen—
The queen weeps for her Darnley?

THROGMORTON

Madame—

ELIZABETH

Ah, yes—
She'll weep and wear black—it becomes
her. A second time
She's a widow now. And she's borne a
child. She begins
To wear a little, no doubt? She must pon-
der now
What costumes may become her?

THROGMORTON

Nay, truly, your Grace,
I'd say she charms as ever.

ELIZABETH

Would you say so?
But she weeps and puts on mourning?

THROGMORTON

No, madame, Bothwell
And the queen are friends again—or more
than that.
They'd be married already, I think, only
Moray's against it
And the earls behind him.

ELIZABETH

Now in my day and time
I have known fools and blockheads, but
never, I swear,
In such numbers as among these Scotch
earls. Moray's against it?
Against the queen's marriage with Bothwell?

BURGHLEY

Your Majesty—
If she were to marry Bothwell—we've op-
posed that, too,
And even prevented it.

ELIZABETH

Aye, times have changed,
And we change along with them. She loves
this Bothwell?
It's a great love—a queen's love?

THROGMORTON

It is indeed.
A madness, almost.

ELIZABETH

Yes, yes—and it's well sometimes
To be mad with love, and let the world
  burn down
In your own white flame. One reads this in
  romances—
Such a love smokes with incense; oh, and
  it's grateful
In the nostrils of the gods! Now who
  would part them
For considerations of earth? Let them have
  this love
This little while—let them bed and board
  together—
Drink it deep, be happy—aye—

BURGHLEY

Madame, this Bothwell's
No man to play with, if they marry she'll
  crown him king—

ELIZABETH

You did well to ride fast, Throgmorton!
  Turn now
And ride as fast back again; you can sleep
  later
When we're old and the years are empty.—
  And tell my lord Moray
If he'd keep me a friend, let his sister
  marry Bothwell—
Tell him to favor it—hurry it.

BURGHLEY

And with Bothwell king
Do you think to conquer Mary?

ELIZABETH

Send next to John Knox,
But do this cleverly, giving Knox evidence
That Bothwell slew Darnley with the
  queen's connivance

And they bed together in blood. Have you
  wit enough
To see this well done?

THROGMORTON

I think so, Majesty.

ELIZABETH

See to it.
Who will deny that Bothwell murdered
  Darnley
When he lives with the queen, and enjoys
  the fruits? Or who
Will credit Bothwell's denial? Your brain,
  my Burghley!
Where do you wear it, or what has it har-
  dened into
That you're so easily gulled?

BURGHLEY

But is it wise
To make a false accusation? This project
  hangs
By a thread. Make but one error and we
  shall lose
Whatever we've gained.

ELIZABETH

Go and do these things—
They are to marry—we sanction it—let
  none oppose it—
She refused him before when he could
  have saved her—
She'll take him now when it's fatal—Let
  her have this love
This little while—we grant her that—then
  raise
The winds against them—rouse the clans,
  cry vengeance
On their guilty sleep and love—I say with-
  in
This year at the very farthest, there's no
  more queen
Than king in Scotland!

Curtain

SCENE III

SCENE: *A hall in Dunbar Castle. A* SENTINEL *is at his post near the outer gate, another at the guard-room door. There is a step on the cobbles outside. The* FIRST SENTINEL *swings round to the gate.*

JAMIE

(*Outside*). Drop your point, man. Ye ken
me.

FIRST SENTINEL

Eh, Jamie. What is it?

JAMIE

I'm late. It was tough getting through. The
queen's taken prisoner. Her army's gone.

FIRST SENTINEL

Nay! And Bothwell?

JAMIE

Bothwell's free yet. Free and able to fight.
We're to put the castle in posture of defence. Where's the sergeant?

FIRST SENTINEL

Call Graeme.

SECOND SENTINEL

Graeme!—I told you this was no lucky
battle to be in.

FIRST SENTINEL

Says John Knox!
(GRAEME *enters*.)

JAMIE

I've orders for the guard. We're to man the
walls and be ready on the gates.

GRAEME

It goes that way?
(BEATON *enters from the stair*.)

JAMIE

That way and worse.
(*They turn toward the gate*.)

BEATON

Jamie, what brings you?

JAMIE

Orders, lass.

BEATON

Quick, tell me!

JAMIE

It goes badly with us, lass.
(LORD HUNTLEY *enters*.)

BEATON

My lord—

HUNTLEY

There's to be a parley here. Make ready for
it.

JAMIE

Watch that outer post.
(*The* SENTINELS *go out*.)

BEATON

A parley—the battle's over?

HUNTLEY

Aye, over and done. This is Moray's kingdom now.

BEATON

And the queen?

HUNTLEY

The queen's a prisoner, lass. My men have
deserted, her own men turned against her.

BEATON

My lord, you'll forgive me, but how could
that be?

HUNTLEY

This was John Knox's battle, lady. The
auld limmer took a stance on a hill some
half-mile to windward, and there he stood
haranguing like the angel Gabriel, swearing Bothwell killed Darnley to have the
queen. And the queen's men listened to
him, the psalm-singing red-beards, and
then turned and made her prisoner and de-
livered her up to Lord Moray.

GRAEME

Bothwell's returning.

JAMIE

Upstairs with you, lass.
(BEATON *goes up the lower stair*.)

GRAEME

Shall I set the guard?

HUNTLEY

Wait a moment.
(BOTHWELL *enters*.)

BOTHWELL

We're not through yet, my lord. You'll
stand by me?

HUNTLEY

Aye,
If it's any use. One may rally an army fly-
ing.
But one that flies toward the enemy and
makes friends—

BOTHWELL

Who spoke of rallying? They won by
treachery,
And we'll treat them some of the same!
(*To* JAMIE.) There were ninety men
Left to guard the castle! They're here still?

JAMIE

Aye, sir.

BOTHWELL

They're under
Lord Huntley's orders while this parley's
on.
Tell them to be ready. He'll join you.

JAMIE

Aye.
(*He goes into the guard-room.*)

BOTHWELL

Sergeant, take the men you need and guard
that arch—
Let no one enter but the lords themselves.

GRAEME

Aye, my lord.
(*He goes out by the arch.*)

BOTHWELL

I'll talk with these lords, and if they listen
to reason
They may keep their mangy lives, but if
they refuse
To release the queen and give her back her
kingdom
Then hell's their home! Watch my arm,
and hark
For my sword on steel. They're outnum-
bered three to one
In this court.

HUNTLEY

Kill them?

BOTHWELL

Cut their throats
If you like that better.

HUNTLEY

That's plain murder.

BOTHWELL

Right,
And if they say no they've earned it.

HUNTLEY

And we'd die, too.

BOTHWELL

Why, it might be we would. But I'd stake
more
On our living long with them dead. If the
queen's deposed
Then I've lived long enough, and so have
you.
Will you gamble with me?

HUNTLEY

I will.
(*They shake hands. A trumpet sounds outside.*)

BOTHWELL

Wait for the signal.
My sword on steel.
(HUNTLEY *goes into the guard-room. The
voices of the Lords are heard outside.*)

MORTON

(*Outside*). Go carefully now. Not too fast.

MORAY

Aye, you're the man to say that.

MORTON

Let Maitland speak.
(*They enter; one or two bow ironically.*)

BOTHWELL

You may drop these scrapings. We know
what we think of each other!

MORTON

And that's true too!

MORAY

We have little to gain, Lord Bothwell,

By a conference with you. The battle is
ours. The queen
Is prisoner to us. But to spare ourselves further bloodshed
And spare you bloodshed, we grant this
respite, and ask
That you surrender without conditions.

BOTHWELL

No.
No, I thank you. Moreover if your tongue's
To be foremost in this council, we'll stop
now
And argue the matter outside.

MAITLAND

Be patient, Lord Moray.
We're here to make terms, as you are,
Bothwell. The queen
And you have been defeated. We made
war on you
Because you two were married, and be-
cause she planned
To make you king.

BOTHWELL

You make war on us
Like the pack of lying hounds you are, by
swearing
In public and in court that we killed Darnley
So that we might marry! You know where
that guilt lies.

MORAY

Who killed Darnley
We care not. Let the courts decide it.

BOTHWELL

It was you that killed him!
And you fight us bearing false witness!

MORAY

You wanted him dead.

BOTHWELL

I grant it. I wanted him dead. You killed
him and managed
To shift the wight on me. You've won with
that lie,
May your mouths rot out with it! And now
what do you want—
What do you ask of us?

MAITLAND

First, that you leave Scotland.

BOTHWELL

That's easily said;
What else?

MAITLAND

Why, next, that the queen should delegate
Her powers to the lords of the council,
those you see
Before you—

BOTHWELL

Aye, I see them.

MAITLAND

And bind herself
To act with our consent only.

BOTHWELL

No more?

MAITLAND

No more.

BOTHWELL

Then here are my conditions; I will leave,
And trouble you no more, if you pledge
your word
That the queen's to keep her throne and
her power intact,
Without prejudice to her rights. But if you
dare
Encroach one inch on her sovereignty,
guard your gates,
For I'll be at them!

MORTON

Aye, you make your terms!

BOTHWELL

Aye, I make mine; defeated, I still make
mine—
And you'll do well to heed them. I shall
want leave also
To see the queen for a moment.

MORAY

You know our answer.

BOTHWELL

Then look to yourselves!
(*He lays a hand on his sword.*)

MAITLAND

Look now. Bothwell.
It's you I rebel against. I'd lend no hand
In this company if the queen were to rule
  alone,
And I've said as much to Lord Moray.

MORTON

I speak for myself,
And say no to it.

MORAY

And I.

BOTHWELL

You've wanted my earldom,
Lord Moray. Well, you may have it. I'll
  make it over.
You shall choose a new earl of Bothwell.
I'll disband my army.
And threaten you no more. But on condition
The queen reigns here as before.

MORAY

We'll make our conditions—
We have no time for yours.

BOTHWELL

My lines are not broken.
I'll try conclusions yet, and you'll not sleep
  easy
While I'm within these borders!

MAITLAND

Take his terms,
My Moray.

MORAY

Are we to fight a war and win
And toss the spoils away?

BOTHWELL

Find some agreement,
For I'm in haste, and if you say no to me
I've other plans!

ERSKINE

Bothwell's been our one weapon
Against the queen, Lord Moray. I believe
  it's wisdom
To banish him, but remember the queen's
  a queen

And it's dangerous to touch her. When he's
  gone
You'll have no cause against her.

MORAY

Why, damn you all!

MORTON

Let him go, and leave her the throne.

MORAY

And even Morton.

MORTON

Gad, I want no long wars,
I'm a married man. Send him on his way!
He leaves his earldom.

BOTHWELL

Then this sword stays in the scabbard
And lucky for all of you. Do you give your
  pledge?

MAITLAND

I give my pledge, Lord Bothwell, for all
  here present.
We have not rebelled against the queen,
  and will not
If you are banished.

BOTHWELL

Then give me leave to speak
Alone with her.

MAITLAND

With the queen?

BOTHWELL

Aye, for a moment.

MORAY

No.

MAITLAND

There's no harm in that, Moray.

ERSKINE

We'll wait in the courtyard.
It's day and we have orders to give.

MORTON

Gordon and Douglas,
You won't be needed. Intercept Lord Hunt-
  ley's men
While there's yet time.

MAITLAND

The queen is here, Lord Bothwell,
And will be free to see you.
(*The Lords go out. After a moment's
pause,* QUEEN MARY *comes to the door—a
soldier on either side. The guards retire,
leaving* MARY *and* BOTHWELL *alone.*)

MARY

Thank God you're safe!

BOTHWELL

And you are safe, my queen, safe and set
  free
And may keep your kingdom.

MARY

At what price?

BOTHWELL

They've made
A bargain with me. God knows whether
  they'll keep it,
But I think they will, for Maitland gave
  his word,
And he's been honest.

MARY

What bargain? You've sacrificed
Yourself for this. What have you offered?

BOTHWELL

Nothing
To weigh against what you'll keep. I've
  given my earldom—
That's a trifle to what we save.

MARY

You shall have it back,
And more to put with it.

BOTHWELL

No. I've accepted exile.
I'm to leave the kingdom.

MARY

Why, then, I'm exiled too.
I'm your wife and I love you, Bothwell.

BOTHWELL

The bargain's made.
You may keep your crown without me but
  not with me.
Do you abdicate your throne? What's left?

MARY

Call in
The men, of your guard, cut our way
  through and ride!
They'll never head us! We can rouse the
  north,
Ask help from France and England, re-
  turn with an army
They dare not meet!

BOTHWELL

You'd raise no army, Marie.
You forget what a drag I am on you. The
  north
Is sullen as the south toward you and me.
What's left we must do apart.

MARY

What if we lost?
At the worst we'd have each other.

BOTHWELL

And do you vision the end of that?
A woman who was a queen, a man who
  was
The earl, her husband, but fugitives, put
  to it
To ask for food and lodging, enemies
On every road; they weary, heartsick, turn-
  ing,
At last on each other with reproaches, she
  saying:
I was a queen, would be one now but for
  you,
And he, I have lost my earldom.

MARY

I betrayed you once
And betrayed my love, but I learned by
  that; I swear
Though it cost my kingdom, not again!

BOTHWELL

If you wish
To thrive, break that oath, betray me, be-
  tray your love,
Give me up forever—for you know as I
  know
We lose together. God knows what we'll
  ever win
Apart.

MARY

Nothing. Oh, Bothwell, the earth goes
  empty.
What worse could happen than parting?

BOTHWELL

Can I stay?
This once for the last I can save you from
yourself,
And me. There's something wills it. I go
alone.
This is your kingdom. Rule it.

MARY

You must not surrender
They'd serve you as they served Darnley.

BOTHWELL

I'll not surrender.
I'll see to my own banishment. find my
guard,
Force my way out, and go.

MARY

We must say good-bye?

BOTHWELL

Aye, girl, we've spent what time we had,
And I know not when I'll see you. Let's
have no pretense
Unworthy of us. It's likely we'll not meet
again
On this same star.

MARY

God help me and all women
Here in this world, and all men. Fair fall
all chances
The heart can long for—and let all women
and men
Drink deep while they can their happiness.
It goes fast
And never comes again. Mine goes with
you,
Youth, and the fund of dreams, and to lie a
while
Trusted, in arms you trust. We're alone,
alone,
Alone—even while we lie there we're alone,
For it's false. It will end. Each one dies
alone.

BOTHWELL

I'll come
If I can. We've loved well, lass, could love
better.
We've had but the broken fragment of a
year
And whenever I've touched you, something
that broods above us

Has made that touch disaster. This is not
my choice.
Lest I bring you utter ruin we must wait,
Wait better times and luck. I'll come again
If I can.

MARY

Yes, if you can. Aye, among all tides
And driftings of air and water it may be
Some dust that once was mine will touch
again
Dust that was yours. I'll not bear it! Oh,
God, I'll not bear it!
Take me with you! Let us be slaves and
pick
Our keep from kitchen middens and leav-
ings! Let us
Quarrel over clouts and fragments, but not
apart—
Bothwell, that much we could have!

BOTHWELL

Is there refuge in this world for you
And me together? Go far as we could, is
there one
Turfed roof where we'd not be reminded
of good days
And end in bitterness? Face these lords
like a queen
And rule like a queen. I'd help you if I
could
But I'm no help. You must meet them now.

MARY

Yes. I'll meet them
Can you break your way through? They're
watching!

BOTHWELL

It's a chance.
Huntley! Huntley!

HUNTLEY

(*Outside*). I'm here.

BOTHWELL

We ride at once
For Stirling. Be ready for a fight

HUNTLEY

We're ready.

BOTHWELL

I must take my moment.

MARY

I know.

BOTHWELL

Good-bye, sweet, but if they wrong you—
if you ever need me,
Look for me back.
(*He kisses her, and goes.*)

MARY

Good-bye. To our two worlds.
(*There is a cry beyond the guard-room:
"*BOTHWELL, *it's* BOTHWELL!" *The alarm is
taken up by the men at the gate, who call:
"On guard there! Pistol him! Mount and
after him! Ride, you devils! On guard!
Drop that portcullis! He's gone!" There is
a sound of running feet from the gate to
the other side of the stage.* MARY *stands
facing the guard-room door.* GORDON *and
*DOUGLAS *run in through the arch.*)

DOUGLAS

Through the guard-room!

GORDON

He'll be over the wall—

DOUGLAS

Out of the way, madame—

GORDON

Nay, it's the queen—

DOUGLAS

Will you let us pass?

MARY

I guard this door, Lord Douglas.
You'll go the long way round!

GORDON

Your pardon, your majesty.
(*He bows.* BEATON *appears on the stairway.
LORDS MORTON, MORAY *and* MAITLAND *en-
ter.*)

MORTON

This was hardly well done, your majesty.

MARY

Take care whom you question, sir.

MORAY

You've sent Bothwell off!
That was your ruse!

MARY

Lord Bothwell will leave Scotland.
That was what you wanted.
(*Enter* LORD ERSKINE.)

MORAY

He's gone?

ERSKINE

Clean away!

MAITLAND

Madame, there was some understanding
You two would remain here.

MARY

None that I know of.

MORTON

Eh, god, he'll wish he had.
(*JOHN KNOX *appears in the archway.*)

MARY

Remove that man from my presence! Is
every stranger
Free to enter my courts?

KNOX

Though you be a queen
And have faith in thy gods and idols, yet
in this day
It will not staunch nor avail! Bid the sea
remove
From the castle front, and gnaw it no
more, as soon
Will it obey thee. Pluck down the whore!
Pluck her down,
This contamination of men!

MARY

Maitland, if there's to be counsel here, send
out
This preacher and his ravings!

MAITLAND

He may stay, for me.

MORAY

Madame, collect what necessities you re-
quire.
You will change your residence.

MARY

That is at my will, I think.

MORTON

Do you think so?

MAITLAND

You are to be lodged
In Holyroodhouse for the time.

MARY

I am to be lodged—
And your faith? You pledged your faith
and word—all of you—
To leave my power untouched, leave me
my throne
If Bothwell and I were parted.

MAITLAND

We'll keep it
When Lord Bothwell's surrendered to us.

MARY

Go out and take him!
Take him if you can! But for your queen,
I warn you, never since there were kings
and queens
In Scotland, has a liegeman laid his hand
On my line without regret!

MORTON

We'll take care of that.

MARY

My lords, if I go with you, expect no pardon,
No clemency; I have friends, this farce will
end.

Once more, then, leave me in peace
I have used you royally. Use me so.

MAITLAND

What you need,
Gather it quickly.

MARY

This is betrayal at once
Of your word and sovereign.

MORTON

We know that.
(*A pause.*)

MARY

I need nothing.
I am a prisoner, Beaton. Come after me
To Holyroodhouse. I may have my own
rooms there, perhaps?

MAITLAND

Yes, madame.

MARY

You show great courtesy. For a liar and
traitor.
You lied to us, a black and level lie!
Blackest and craftiest! It was you we believed!

MORAY

Aye, sister. It was that we counted on.

MARY

Aye, brother.
(MARY *turns from* MAITLAND *to* MORAY, *then
walks to the archway and goes out.*)

Curtain

ACT THREE

SCENE: *A room in Carlisle Castle, in England. There are two windows at the right, both
barred, a door at the rear and another, the hall-door, at the left. It is a prison room, but
furnished scantily now for the queen's habitation. It is evening, but still light.*

MARY *sits at one of the windows, leaning her head against the bars.*

BEATON *is leaning over a table where* FLEMING *has unrolled a map.*

FLEMING

We came this way, through Cockermouth,
and then took hired horses.

BEATON

If I had a thousand maps I couldna tell you
how I came. Jamie's acquent wi' the drov

ers and all the back ways. Seton and Livingstone, poor things, they're pining away
back in Edinburgh Town.

FLEMING

We might be as well off in Edinburgh ourselves, as it turns out. We'd looked forward
to England for a free country, and strained
toward it till our shoulders ached, trying
to help the boat through the water. And
here we are, and there's bars on the windows.

BEATON

But whose prisoners are we, Fleming?

FLEMING

I would I knew. It's been a month now,
and all I can tell you is we're prisoners, for
we cannot leave.

BEATON

There's some mistake, Fleming.

FLEMING

Aye, if it was a mistake, like, would it last
a month? It's heartbreaking to escape one
jailer and walk into the arms of another.

MARY

When does the guard change, Fleming?

FLEMING

At ten, madame.

MARY

You're certain Jamie will come?

BEATON

Unless he's taken or dead, Your Majesty.
He's true as one can have in a lad.

MARY

But they may unmask him.

BEATON

It's true, they may.

FLEMING

Ye've more friends than a few in this
castle, madame. They'd let us know if summat went wrong.

MARY

What friends?

FLEMING

The two guards that go on for evening
watch.

MARY

I fear they can't help much.

FLEMING

They can always bring us news.

BEATON

And you've more friends than that, Your
Majesty. Here and everywhere. As I came
through the back roads I heard talk of you
everywhere. I think they love their queen
better now than before, now that she's shut
away unjustly.

MARY

Do you think so?

BEATON

From what I heard I'd say the lords had
worked their own ruin when they first betrayed you. If they could hear the buzzing
against them they'd sleep badly there
nights. And who rules Scotland now? Moray has no right to it, and nobody can give
him the right save your own self.

MARY

Aye, that's so. He'll come begging yet.

BEATON

And for what he'll never have.

MARY

They've taken my son from me, though. If
I have friends I would they'd hurry.
(She turns toward the window.)
God knows what Elizabeth means.

FLEMING

You'll hear from Bothwell tonight, madame, or hear of him. I'm certain of it.
(A WATCHMAN calls outside.)

WATCHMAN

Ten o'clock, and all well. All well.

BEATON

Ten o'clock and still light.

FLEMING

The days grow longer and longer.

MARY

They've grown so long that each is the whole time between a birth and a death—and yet they go so fast, too, that I catch at them with my hand. So fast that I watch the evening light jealously, like a last candle burning. This is life, too, Beaton, here in this prison, and it goes from us quite as much as though we were free. We shall never see these same days again.

FLEMING

And little will I want to.

MARY

But suppose you were to spend all your life in prisons? Might not one grow to love even prison-days—as better than none?

BEATON

We shall have better, though. These are the worst we shall have, and I think the last of them.
(*There is a rasping at the door.*)
You hear?—the signal—
(*There is a silence.*)

FLEMING

Nay, not yet.
(*Another pause.*)

BEATON

It's ten, and more.

FLEMING

If we must wait again, then we must wait. He'll come at the latest, tomorrow.

MARY

(*Rising and pacing near her window*). But what could Elizabeth mean? What could she mean? She is my friend—over and over she writes she is my friend, I am her dear cousin, her sister sovereign, that she suffers when I suffer, that she would confine me on no pretext if it were not to secure me against my own enemies! Enemies! What enemies have I in her kingdom? What right has she to imprison a sovereign who takes sanctuary in England?

FLEMING

Has any one ever known Elizabeth's mind on any subject?

MARY

Writes, too, that she will come to see me, writes again to put it off, writes to say she cannot bear the week to pass without reassuring me of her good love.

BEATON

And yet I believe if all else fails Elizabeth will be found a friend and a good one at the end. If only for her own interest.

MARY

It may still be that she goes, in her own muddled and devious way, about the business of aiding me. It still may be.
(*There is a rasping at the door again.*)

BEATON

Yes?
(*The door opens a crack, a chain clanging.*)

JAMIE

(*Outside*). I may enter?

BEATON

Aye, come in.
(JAMIE *steps in, closing the door.*)

JAMIE

(*Bonnet in hand*). Your Majesty!

MARY

Good evening, Jamie.

JAMIE

Ye'll forgive me. I was not sure I could jouk in, for the captain loitered about. However, the lad Mark keeps a look-out, and warns me if there's footsteps.

BEATON

Was there a messenger through, Jamie?

JAMIE

Aye, I'll be quick, for I must, though a man hates to be quick wi' ill news. There's been a messenger, true enough, coming down wi' the drovers, as we cam'—and his tale is there was a battle at the Little Minch Ma'am; it went badly for Bothwell, if the man says sooth, for he was defeated and taken.

MARY

Bothwell taken?

JAMIE

Aye, madame. Aye, but there's some good, too. Kirkaldy of Grange has come over to Your Majesty's side and makes his threats against Moray.

MARY

But Bothwell, Bothwell was taken? How?

JAMIE

That's the bare sum of it, madame. Just that he was prisoner to the lords. Only Kirkaldy has said Bothwell should be freed, and that he will see to it.

MARY

It's little comfort.

JAMIE

Aye, so I feared. Though Kirkaldy was their best general, and they'll miss him.

MARY

I could have used him once.

JAMIE

And now, if you'll pardon me, I must go. I had little liking to come—it's sore bad manners to leave folk wi' heavy hearts—

MARY

Nay, run no risk—only come again if there's any tidings.

JAMIE

Yes, Your Majesty, and I pray God they be better.
(*He turns.*)

BEATON

Jamie.
(*There is a sharp rap at the door.*)

JAMIE

Aye?
(BEATON *goes up to him.*)
Nay, lass, it's good just to see thee, but we'll not kiss afore Her Majesty.
(*The rap again.*)
It's for me. Keep thee, and all here.
(*He opens the door and goes out, closing it softly. The chain clanks. There is silence.*)

MARY

It's this that drives one mad, Beaton, to know
That on one certain day, at a certain hour,
If one had but chosen well, he'd have stood beside me
In a land all mine and his. Choosing wrong, I bring him
To fight a long war for me, and lose, bow his shoulders
To a castle keep.

FLEMING

They'll not hold him long.

MARY

And that's
To remember too. He's not a man to hold
Easily, no, nor hold at all. I've seen him
When they thought him trapped, and well caught. His face goes cold,
Stern, and morgue under his morion. While he lives
And I live, they'll not jail us two apart,
Nor keep our due from us. Aye, it's something to love,
Even late, even bitterly, where it's deserved. Kirkaldy
Throws his weight on our side. There'll be others, too. Oh, Bothwell,
You've been my one hope! Bring me back to mind,
Now, as I bring you back!
(*The chains of the door are undone, and the door opens. A* GUARD *steps in.*)

GUARD

Your Majesty,
Lord Ruthven desires to see you.

MARY

Lord Ruthven's in Scotland.

GUARD

No, madame, he's here.

MARY

Why, I will see Lord Ruthven.
Yes, let him come in.
(*The door swings wider and* YOUNG RUTHVEN *enters. He bows.*)
Sir, there've been days,
Not so far back when I'd have shifted somehow

To do without your face, or any visage
Among a certain congeries of lords
Of which you're one. Perhaps I'm tamed a
trace
Sitting mewed at my window, for I'd ac-
cept
Any visitor from Scotland, bailiffs and
hang-men
Not excluded, I'm that lonely.

RUTHVEN

Madame,
You hold against me much that was not
my own.
I'm of a party, and one must swim or go
down
With those of his interest.

MARY

Do you come now to see me
In your own person, then, or as represent-
ing
Those sharks you swam with last?

RUTHVEN

Why, Your Majesty,
It may be we're sharks. My mind's not
made up. But I've come,
If you'll pardon me—and this is more truth,
I think,
Than I'm supposed to say—because the
lords
Who now hold Scotland had more hope
you'd see me
Than any the others.

MARY

That's frank.

RUTHVEN

And I lend myself
To the embassy because, as things drift at
home,
We verge on the rocks there. You are still
queen of Scotland,
Yet you don't rule, and can't rule, being
here,
A prisoner—and the upshot is we're not
ruled.
There's anarchy in the air. It's necessary
That some approach be made between you
and your brother
Before there's anarchy in the streets.

BEATON

We were saying
That he'd come begging.

MARY

What does my brother ask—
This good brother of mine?

RUTHVEN

That goes beyond
My mission. To be frank still, I'm sent be
fore
To ask whether you will see him.

MARY

Let him ask my jailers
Whether I may be seen.

RUTHVEN

He has asked already, madame.
The request is granted.

MARY

Lord Moray is with you?

RUTHVEN

He is waiting.

MARY

Why, this is an honor. And others too, no
doubt?
A shoal of them?

RUTHVEN

Madame, as you have supposed
They are all here.

MARY

It will please me vastly to view them,
If only to know from them who gave per-
mission
To see me. For I swear, I guess not so far
Whose prisoner I am, or who keeps my
jail. I've moithered
Over this a good deal.

RUTHVEN

I may call them?

MARY

If you'll be so good.
(RUTHVEN *bows and goes out past the*
GUARD.)

Is it you, sir, who chain my door
So assiduously at night?

GUARD

No, madame, the turn-key
Goes the rounds at twelve.

MARY

Will you ask him, then.
To make a thought less jangling if he can?
We try to sleep, you see, and these chimes
   at midnight
Are not conducive to slumber.

GUARD

He shall be told;
I'm very sorry, Your Majesty.

MARY

Thank you.
(MORTON *and* MORAY *come in. and behind
them* MAITLAND *and* DOUGLAS. RUTHVEN *re-
enters with* THROGMORTON.)
Gentlemen,
I greet you. You are all here, I see, the
   whole
Blood-thirsty race. But we lack John Knox.
   Now, surely,
John Knox should be with you.

MORAY

Have your jest, my sister. For us
We're not here for jesting.

MARY

Oh, I'd have sworn you weren't.
You're no harbinger of merriment, my bro-
   ther,
Nor of good fortune. The corbies from the
   wood
Presage more of that. And here's the Lord
   Throgmorton
Presses in among you! It should be a good
   day
When I'm crossed by this constellation!

THROGMORTON

We pray it will,
Your Majesty, and that things may be iron-
   ed out clean
That have grieved us all.

MARY

Oh, do you know of grief,
You who may take your meals in your own
   wide halls

And walk in the rainy air? I had thought
   that grieving
Was something found behind bars.

MAITLAND

This has lasted too long,
This imprisonment, Your Majesty, and was
   never
To any purpose. We come to offer you
Release, and speedily.

MARY

The diplomat always, Maitland.
Always the secret thought glancing behind
The quick-silver tongue. You come to ask
   for much
And give little for it, as ever.

MORAY

We come to ask
For what we have.

MARY

There, now it's brutally said,
In my brother's plain-Scotch way, spoken
   plainly out of
His plain Scotch face. He comes to ask, he
   says,
For what he has, and he makes no doubt
   he'll get it.
What is it you have, dear brother, and if
   you have it
Why ask for it?

MAITLAND

Will Your Majesty give me leave
To rehearse a brief history that may weary
   you
Since you know it?

MARY

It will weary me, but go on.

MAITLAND

Forgive me: Your Majesty broke from prison in Scotland
And fled to England. This action was tan-
   tamount
To abandoning your throne.

MARY

Indeed it was not.
I came here for aid against you.

MAITLAND

We will pass that point.

MARY

Do. There's nothing gives me more pleasure, Lord Maitland,
Than passing a point.

MAITLAND

Then am I delighted to render
Your Majesty pleasure. Your wit is sharper
than mine.
But to proceed: You were taken prisoner
in England—

MARY

By whom, Lord Maitland—will you tell
me that?
Who holds me here?

MAITLAND

That I'm not free to answer.
It remains that you're a prisoner, and that
your realm
Is governed only by makeshift. Your son,
the prince James—

MARY

Aye, what of him? My lords, I beg of you,
Whatever you must do, or think you must
do,
To secure yourselves, he's but a babe, re-
member.
I can stand up and fight you for myself,
But use my child more kindly.

MAITLAND

The prince James,
Is well, and well cared for, and will be.
The succession
Depends on him. We plan to make him
king.
Your absence makes this necessary.

MARY

My absence
Is not permanent, I hope. I am queen of
Scotland
And have not abdicated, nor do I intend
To abdicate.

MORTON

Will you tell us what you think
To find, should you return?

MARY

If I return
As I intend, I shall not find you there,
Lord Morton, if you're wise. The country's
fickle.
For you as it was for me. Now they've
pushed their queen
Aside, they begin to wonder if they were
not wrong.
And wonder too if they profit by the ex
change,
And give you side-long looks.

MAITLAND

If it's still in your mind
That you might win your throne back,
ponder on this:
The lord of the isles has given you up, the
north
Is solidly with us, Bothwell has broken
faith—

MARY

Aye?

MAITLAND

For the good of the kingdom, to secure
your son
His right to the throne, we ask you tonight
to sign
Your abdication, let us take it back with
us.

MARY

Yes,
But I catch you in two lies. Kirkaldy of
Grange
Has come over to me; you have taken Both-
well prisoner,
But before he fights on your side you'll rot
in the damp
Under Edinburgh castle, and he'll see you
do it!

MAITLAND

Madame,
You've been misinformed.

MARY

I've been lied to and by you
Specifically! Let me rehearse for you
A history you may recall, you that stand be-
fore me:
It was you killed Rizzio, and made capital
of it
To throw discredit on me. It was you

MARY

Killed Darnley, and then threw the weight
of that
On Bothwell, saying through John Knox
that I lived
With my husband's murderer. It was you
that promised
To give me fealty if Bothwell and I were
parted,
And then cast me into prison! I escaped,
As the truth will escape about you, and
when it's known
My people will drive you out. What you
ask of me
I refuse it, finally! I will not abdicate,
Not to this off-scum that's boiled up around
My throne to dirty me! Not now and not
ever!
(*The Lords are silent for a moment, and
then* MORAY *nods an assent to* MAITLAND.)

MAITLAND

Your Majesty, you asked me a moment
since
Who held you prisoner here. I cannot answer
Still, but say there's another and higher
judge
Must pass on these charges of yours.

MARY

Nay, I know that.

MAITLAND

Oh, an earthly judge, Your Majesty, and
yet
High enough, I think. We wish you good
night.

MARY

Good night.
(*The Lords go out.* MARY *stands unmov-
ing, watching the door. After a pause the*
GUARD *pushes the door back and with-
draws.* ELIZABETH *comes to the doorway.*
MARY *looks at her questioningly.*)
I have seen but a poor likeness, and yet I
believe
This is Elizabeth.

ELIZABETH

I am Elizabeth.
May we be alone together?
(*At a sign from* MARY *the* MAIDS *go out the
rear door.* ELIZABETH *enters and the hall-
door swings to behind her.*)

MARY

I had hoped to see you.
When last you wrote you were not sure.

ELIZABETH

If I've come
So doubtfully and tardigrade, my dear,
And break thus in upon you, it's not for
lack
Of thinking of you. Rather because I've
thought
Too long, perhaps, and carefully. Then at
last
It seemed if I saw you near, and we talked
as sisters
Over these poor realms of ours, some light
might break
That we'd never see apart.

MARY

Have I been so much
A problem?

ELIZABETH

Have you not? When the winds blow
down
The houses, and there's a running and arm-
ing of men,
And a great cry of praise and blame, and
the center
Of all this storm's a queen, she beautiful—
As I see you are—

MARY

Nay—

ELIZABETH

Aye, with the Stuart mouth
And the high forehead and French ways
and thoughts—
Well, we must look to it.—Not since that
Helen
We read of in dead Troy, has a woman's
face
Stirred such a confluence of air and waters
To beat against the bastions. I'd thought
you taller,
But truly, since that Helen, I think there's
been
No queen so fair to look on.

MARY

You flatter me.

ELIZABETH

It's more likely envy. You see this line

Drawn down between my brows? No
  wash or ointments
Nor wearing of straight plasters in the
  night
Will take that line away. Yet I'm not much
  older
Than you, and had looks, too, once.

MARY

I had wished myself
For a more regal beauty such as yours,
More fitting for a queen.

ELIZABETH

Were there not two verses
In a play I remember:
    Brightness falls from the air;
    Queens have died young and fair—?
They must die young if they'd die fair, my
  cousin,
Brightness falls from them, but not from
  you yet; believe me,
It's envy, not flattery.

MARY

Can it be—as I've hoped—
Can it be that you come to me as a friend—
Meaning me well?

ELIZABETH

Would you have me an enemy?

MARY

I have plenty to choose among as enemies—
And sometimes, as your word reached out
  to me
Through embassies, entangled with men's
  tongues,
It has seemed you judged me harshly, even
  denying
My right to a place beside you. But now
  you are here,
And a woman like myself, fearing as I do,
With the little dark fears of a woman, the
  creeping of age
On a young face, I see truer—I think I see
  truer.
And that this may be some one to whom I
  can reach a hand
And feel a clasp, and trust it. A woman's
  hand,
Stronger than mine in this hour, willing to
  help.
If that were so—

ELIZABETH

Aye.

MARY

Of, if that were so.
I have great power to love! Let them buzz
  forever
Between us, these men with messages and
  lies,
You'll find me still there, and smiling, and
  open-hearted,
Unchanging while the cusped hills wear
  down!

ELIZABETH

(*Smiling*).
Nay, pledge
Not too much, my dear, for in these un-
  certain times
It's slippery going for all of us. I, who seem
  now
So firm in my footing, well I know one
  mis-step
Could make me a most unchancy friend.
  If you'd keep
Your place on this rolling ball, let the
  mountains slide
And slip to the valleys. Put no hand to
  them
Or they'll pull you after.

MARY

But does this mean you can lend
No hand to me, or I'll pull you down?

ELIZABETH

I say it
Recalling how I came to my throne as you
  did,
Some five or six years before, beset as you
  were
With angry factions — and came there
  young, loving truth,
As you did. This was many centuries since,
Or seems so to me. I'm so old by now
In shuffling tricks and the huckstering of
  souls
For lands and pensions. I learned to play it
  young,
Must learn it or die.—It's thus if you would
  rule;
Give up good faith, the word that goes
  with the heart,
The heart that clings where it loves. Give
  these up, and love
Where your interest lies, and should your
  interest change

Let your love follow it quickly. This is
  queen's porridge,
And however little stomach she has for it
A queen must eat it.

MARY

I, too, Elizabeth,
Have read my Machiavelli. His is a text-
  book
Much studied in the French court. Are you
  serious
To rede me this lesson?

ELIZABETH

You have too loving a heart,
I fear, and too bright a face to be a queen.

MARY

That's not what's charged against me.
  When I've lost
So far it's been because my people believed
I was more crafty than I am. I've been
Traduced as a murderess and adulteress
And nothing I could have said, and noth-
  ing done
Would have warded the blow. What I seek
  now is only
My freedom, so that I may return and
  prove
In open court, and before my witnesses,
That I am guiltless. You are the queen of
  England,
And I am held prisoner in England. Why
  am I held,
And who is it holds me?

ELIZABETH

It was to my interest, child,
To protect you, lest violence be offered to
  a princess
And set a precedent. Is there any one in
  England
Who could hold you against my will?

MARY

Then I ask as a sovereign,
Speaking to you as an equal, that I be
  allowed
To go, and fight my own battles.

ELIZABETH

It would be madness.

MARY

May I not judge of that?

ELIZABETH

See, here is our love!

MARY

If you wish my love and good-will you
  shall have it freely
When I am free.

ELIZABETH

You will never govern, Mary. If I let you
  go
There will be long broils again in Scotland,
  dangers,
And ripe ones, to my peace at home. To be
  fair
To my own people, this must not be.

MARY

Now speak once
What your will is, and what behind it!
  You wish me here,
You wish me in prison—have we come to
  that?

ELIZABETH

It's safer.

MARY

Who do you wish to rule in Scotland,
If not my Stuart line?

ELIZABETH

Have I said, my dear,
That I'd bar the Stuarts from Scotland, or
  bar your reign
If you were there, and reigned there? I say
  only
You went the left way about it, and since
  it's so
And has fallen out so, it were better for
  both our kingdoms
If you remained my guest.

MARY

For how long?

ELIZABETH

Until
The world is quieter.

MARY

And who will rule in my place?

ELIZABETH

Why, who rules now? Your brother.

MARY

He rules by stealth—

ELIZABETH

But all this could be arranged,
Or so I'm told, if your son were to be
crowned king,
And Moray made regent.

MARY

My son in Moray's hands—
Moray in power—

ELIZABETH

Is there any other way?
(*A pause.*)

MARY

Elizabeth—I have been here a long while
Already—it seems so. If it's your policy
To keep me—shut me up—. I can argue
no more—
No—I beg now. There's one I love in the
north.
You know that—and my life's there, my
throne's there, my name
To be defended—and I must lie here dark-
ened
From news and from the sun—lie here im-
paled
On a brain's agony—wondering even some-
times
If I were what they said me—a carrion-
thing
In my desires—can you understand this?—
I speak it
Too brokenly to be understood, but I beg
you
As you are a woman and I am—and our
brightness falls
Soon enough at best—let me go, let me
have my life
Once more—and my dear health of mind
again—
For I rot away here in my mind—in what
I think of myself—some death-tinge falls
over one
In prisons—

ELIZABETH

It will grow worse, not better. I've known
Strong men shut up alone for years—it's
not
Their hair turns white only; they sicken
within

And scourge themselves. If you would
think like a queen
This is no place for you. The brain taints
here
Till all desires are alike. Be advised and
sign
The abdication.

MARY

Stay now a moment. I begin to glimpse
Behind this basilisk mask of yours. It was
this
You've wanted from the first.

ELIZABETH

This that I wanted?

MARY

It was you sent Lord Throgmorton long
ago
When first I'd have married Bothwell. All
this while
Some evil's touched my life at every turn.
To cripple what I'd do. And now—why
now—
Looking on you—I see it incarnate before
me—
It was your hand that touched me. Reach-
ing out
In little ways—here a word, there an ac-
tion—this
Was what you wanted. I thought perhaps
a star—
Wildly I thought it—perhaps a star might
ride
Astray—or a crone that burned an image
down
In wax—filling the air with curses on me
And slander; the murder of Rizzio, Moray
in that
And you behind Moray—the murder of
Darnley, Throgmorton
Behind that too, you with them—and that
winged scandal
You threw at us when we were married.
Proof I have none
But I've felt it—would know it anywhere
—in your eyes—
There—before me.

ELIZABETH

What may become a queen
Is to rule her kingdom. Had you ruled
yours I'd say
She has her ways, I mine. Live and let live
And a merry world for those who have it.
But now

I must think this over—sadness has touched
your brain.
I'm no witch to charm you, make no in-
cantations;
You came here by your own road.

MARY

I see how I came.
Back, back, each step the wrong way, and
each sign followed
As you'd have me go, till the skein picks
up and we stand
Face to face here. It was you forced Both-
well from me—
You there, and always. Oh, I'm to blame in
this, too!
I should have seen your hand!

ELIZABETH

It has not been my use
To speak much or spend my time—

MARY

How could I have been
Mistaken in you for an instant?

ELIZABETH

You were not mistaken.
I am all women I must be. One's a young
girl.
Young and harrowed as you are—one who
could weep
To see you here—and one's a bitterness
At what I have lost and can never have,
and one's
The basilisk you saw. This last stands
guard
And I obey it. Lady, you came to Scotland
A fixed and subtle enemy, more dangerous
To me than you've ever known. This could
not be borne,
And I set myself to cull you out and down,
And down you are.

MARY

When was I your enemy?

ELIZABETH

Your life was a threat to mine, your throne
to my throne,
Your policy a threat.

MARY

How? Why?

ELIZABETH

It was you
Or I. Do you know that? The one of us
must win
And I must always win. Suppose one lad
With a knife in his hand, a Romish lad
who planted
That knife between my shoulders—my
kingdom was yours.
It was too easy. You might not have
wished it.
But you'd take it if it came.

MARY

And you'd take my life
And love to avoid this threat?

ELIZABETH

Nay, keep your life.
And your love, too. The lords have brought
a parchment
For you to sign. Sign it and live.

MARY

If I sign it
Do I live where I please? Go free?

ELIZABETH

Nay, I would you might,
But you'd go to Bothwell, and between you
two
You might be too much for Moray. You'll
live with me
In London. There are other loves, my dear.
You'll find amusement there in the court.
I assure you
It's better than a cell.

MARY

And if I will not sign
This abdication?

ELIZABETH

You've tasted prison. Try
A diet of it.

MARY

And so I will.

ELIZABETH

I can wait.

MARY

And I can wait. I can better wait than you.
Bothwell will fight free again. Kirkaldy
Will fight beside him, and others will
spring up

From these dragon's teeth you've sown.
Each week that passes
I'll be stronger, and Moray weaker.

ELIZABETH

And do you fancy
They'll rescue you from an English prison?
Why,
Let them try it.

MARY

Even that they may do. I wait for Bothwell—
And wait for him here.

ELIZABETH

Where you will wait, bear in mind,
Is for me to say. Give up Bothwell, give up
your throne
If you'd have a life worth living.

MARY

I will not.

ELIZABETH

I can wait.

MARY

And will not because you play to lose. This
trespass
Against God's right will be known. The
nations will know it,
Mine and yours. They will see you as I
see you
And pull you down.

ELIZABETH

Child, child, I've studied this gambit
Before I play it. I will send each year
This paper to you. Not signing, you will
step
From one cell to another, step lower always,
Till you reach the last, forgotten, forgotten
of men,
Forgotten among causes, a wraith that cries
To fallen gods in another generation
That's lost your name. Wait then for Both-
well's rescue.
It will never come.

MARY

I may never see him?

ELIZABETH

Never.
It would not be wise.

MARY

And suppose indeed you won
Within our life-time, still looking down
from the heavens
And up from men around us, God's spies
that watch
The fall of great and little, they will find
you out—
I will wait for that, wait longer than a life,
Till men and the times unscroll you, study
the tricks
You play, and laugh, as I shall laugh, being
known
Your better, haunted by your demon,
driven
To death or exile by you, unjustly. Why,
When all's done, it's my name I care for,
my name and heart,
To keep them clean. Win now, take your
triumph now,
For I'll win men's hearts in the end—
though the sifting takes
This hundred years—or a thousand.

ELIZABETH

Child, child, are you gulled
By what men write in histories, this or
that,
And never true? I am careful of my name.
As you are, for this day and longer. It's not
what happens
That matters, no, not even what happens
that's true,
But what men believe to have happened.
They will believe
The worst of you, the best of me, and that
Will be true of you and me. I have seen to
this.
What will be said about us in after-years
By men to come, I control that, being who
I am.
It will be said of me that I governed well,
And wisely, but of you, cousin, that your
life,
Shot through will ill-loves, battened on
lechery, made you
An ensign of evil, that men tore down and
trampled.
Shall I call for the lord's parchment?

MARY

This will be said—?
But who will say it? It's a lie—will be
known as a lie!

ELIZABETH

You lived with Bothwell before Darnley
died,
You and Bothwell murdered Darnley.

MARY

And that's a lie!

ELIZABETH

Your letters, my dear. Your letters to Bothwell prove it.
We have those letters.

MARY

Then they're forged and false!
For I never wrote them!

ELIZABETH

It may be they were forged.
But will that matter, Mary, if they're be-
lieved?
All history is forged.

MARY

You would do this?

ELIZABETH

It is already done.

MARY

And still I win.
A demon has no children, and you have
none,
Will have none, can have none, perhaps.
This crooked track
You've drawn me on, cover it, let it not be
believed
That a woman was a fiend. Yes, cover it
deep,
And heap my infamy over it, lest men peer
And catch sight of you as you were and
are. In myself
I know you to be an eater of dust. Leave
me here
And set me lower this year by year, as you
promise,
Till the last is an oubliette, and my name
inscribed
On the four winds. Still, STILL I win! I
have been
A woman, and I have loved as a woman
loves,
Lost as a woman loses. I have borne a son,
And he will rule Scotland—and England.
You have no heir!
A devil has no children.

ELIZABETH

By God, you shall suffer
For this, but slowly.

MARY

And that I can do. A woman
Can do that. Come, turn the key. I have a
hell
For you in mind, where you will burn and
feel it,
Live where you live, and softly.

ELIZABETH

Once more I ask you,
And patiently. Give up your throne.

MARY

No, devil.
My pride is stronger than yours, and my
heart beats blood
Such as yours has never known. And in
this dungeon,
I win here, alone.

ELIZABETH

(*Turning*). Good night, then.

MARY

Aye, good night.
(ELIZABETH *goes to the door, which opens
before her. She goes out slowly. As the
door begins to close upon her* MARY *calls.*)
Beaton!

ELIZABETH

(*Turning*).
You will not see your maids again,
I think. It's said they bring you news from
the north.

MARY

I thank you for all kindness.
(ELIZABETH *goes out.* MARY *stands for a
moment in thought, then walks to the wall
and lays her hand against the stone, push-
ing outward. The stone is cold, and she
shudders. Going to the window she sits
again in her old place and looks out into
the darkness.*)

Curtain

This is the end of this publication.

Any remaining blank pages are for our book binding
requirements and are blank on purpose.

To search thousands of interesting publications like this one,
please remember to visit our website at:

http://www.kessinger.net

CPSIA information can be obtained at www.ICGtesting.com
Printed in the USA
LVOW08s1715270814

401204LV00017B/1113/P